MY INCREDIBLY WONDERFUL, MISERABLE LIFE

An Anti-Memoir

ADAM NIMOY

Pocket Books
New York   London   Toronto   Sydney

Author's Note

Some of the names and other identifying characteristics of the persons or places included in this memoir have been changed.

 Pocket Books
A Division of Simon & Schuster, Inc.
1230 Avenue of the Americas
New York, NY 10020

First Pocket Books trade paperback edition June 2009

POCKET and colophon are registered trademarks of
Simon & Schuster, Inc.

For information about special discounts for bulk purchases,
please contact Simon & Schuster Special Sales at 1-800-456-6798
or business@simonandschuster.com.

The Simon & Schuster Speakers Bureau can bring authors to your live event. For more information or to book an event, contact the Simon & Schuster Speakers Bureau at 1-866-248-3049 or visit our website at www.simonspeakers.com.

Designed by Elliott Beard
Photo editor: Nancy Nimoy
Photo on page 190 by F. Scott Schafer

Manufactured in the United States of America

10 9 8 7 6 5 4 3 2 1

Library of Congress Cataloging-in-Publication Data

Nimoy, Adam.
    My incredibly wonderful, miserable life: an anti-memoir / by Adam Nimoy.
       p. cm.
1. Nimoy, Leonard—Family. 2. Nimoy, Adam. 3. Children of celebrities—United States—Biography. I. Title.
    PN2287.N55N56 2008
    791.4502'8092—dc22
    [B]   2008014336

ISBN 978-1-4391-2546-5 (pbk)

For Maddy and Jonah

MY INCREDIBLY WONDERFUL, MISERABLE LIFE

TELEPHONE CALL TO MY MOTHER

IT STARTED SEVERAL months ago when I called my mother with the good news.

"Mom, I'm thinking about writing a book."

"Really? What are you going to write about?"

"Me and my wonderful life."

"That's a great idea. You can write about all the people you met and how you used to go to the set with your father and about the time they put the ears on you."

"Mom, I'm not going to write about that."

"What? Why not?"

"Because nobody wants to hear about that crap. I'm going to write about the dark times, about the times when I was down and out, about the times when I could barely survive, like when you and Dad were out of town on some *Star Trek* press junket and I was strung out on the floor of that men's room downtown, when I almost OD'd and was passed out in my own vomit in that stinking men's room with the toilets overflooded and shit everywhere and the glaring lights and the bums and the flies and me on the floor passed out with a needle in my arm." My mother's about to have a heart attack over the phone.

"Tha . . . that . . . that never happened to you!"

"No, Ma, I know. But that's what people want to hear."

POWER LUNCH

I GET UP at 5:45 AM and drive Jonah, my fourteen-year-old son, down to the beach for Surf Club. We get there and meet up with Scott, a middle school teacher who runs the club. While Scott is getting into his wetsuit he asks me what's been going on. I tell him I've been writing my memoirs, covering everything from my recovery from drugs and alcohol to the raising of my teenage kids. I tell him I'm also writing about my attempts to re-create my personal and professional life after the crash and burn of my marriage and my directing career. Scott says this all sounds very interesting and that he knows a literary agent he can put me in touch with if I'm interested. Yeah, I'm interested.

So Scott writes an e-mail to this agent telling him he should meet me because I have an interesting story to tell and that "growing up the son of a celebrity had some funny and touching hardships." I don't know where the hell he got that crap, because I never mentioned anything about that growing-up stuff. Just his sales pitch, I guess, but it worked. Richard, the agent, jumps at the chance, saying he's a "big *Star Trek* fan" and that "Spock is, like, the John Lennon of the group" and that he looks forward to having lunch with me.

The following week, I meet this guy at Factor's Deli on Pico. Richard is tall, well over six feet, which is pretty tall for an agent. He's wearing all black, shirttails out, hip-and-groovy black-framed glasses. We're sitting at a table on the back patio and it's sunny and hot out there. There are umbrellas at each table but it's still cooking. There's a bleached blonde with huge breasts sitting with an older woman at the table behind Richard and she's checking me out, which is totally distracting. Suddenly, I picture the two of us rolling around in bed together—the blonde and me. But I've got to stay focused here because Richard's with a heavyweight agency and I don't want to blow my big chance.

I let him do all the talking: He's thirty-three, was raised in Toluca Lake, and is from a wealthy Jewish family that made their fortune in kosher foods. He was a successful child actor until he grew up and wanted to stop. He went to law school but discovered that people became guarded when he told them he was a lawyer, so he decided not to practice. He managed to get himself into this literary agency and now he wears all black. He's recently married, his wife's an attorney, and they live in Silver Lake. I manage to slip in that I'm also an attorney and that after practicing for seven years, I started directing TV shows. Now I teach filmmaking and raise my teenage children. He tells me the baby-boom generation is like that: We were handed everything on a silver platter and then spent decades trying to "discover ourselves." He says that his generation has been paying the price for that trip of discovery ever since.

Hmmmm.

I'm not quite sure what he means by all that but it kind of sounds insulting. Especially from a child actor-turned-attorney-turned-agent.

And what about that bleached blonde? I mean, what would happen after we finished up in bed? Would she want me to take her to dinner? What if we bumped into my kids? I mean, she's so clearly inappropriate for me, what if we bumped into *anyone*?

Lunch arrives and I refocus on Richard. He takes a couple of bites from his Reuben sandwich, then launches into what he thinks this book should be about. He tells me we should start off with my childhood and what that was like before getting into the *Star Trek* years. Then we'd go into how my life changed after the show started airing and segue into life thereafter with particular attention to the 1970s, when the show became a hit in syndication. He goes on and on about how this story is playing out in his head, about how I can bring a whole new perspective to a phenomenon that's been a pillar of pop culture for more than forty years. And there are dollar signs. I swear I can see dollar signs in his eyes as he explains how he's going to shop me to all the major publishing houses. He thinks he's going to get some bidding war going when he starts sending out the manuscript—to be written by a hired gun I'll be working "closely" with—and that the book will be entitled something catchy, like *My Life with Leonard* or *Son of Spock* or maybe *I Am Not the Son of Spock*.

Then he takes a moment from his grand plans to actually ask me a question.

"So what *was* it like growing up with him as a father? Just tell me like you were telling a therapist at your first session."

Just tell him like I was telling a therapist at my first session.

Hmmmm.

I've got to stop to think about that one.

Richard digs deeper into his Reuben sandwich. I've never had a Reuben. I don't know, the sauerkraut thing never really appealed to me. I'm having turkey and Swiss on rye with Russian dressing. I didn't realize it was a triple-decker and I've been having trouble fitting it into my mouth. I'm kinda losing my appetite now anyway, so I just let it sit there knowing I'm going to be asking for a doggie bag. The blonde is having a salad. Great figure, tight white sweater in eighty-degree heat, pointed white pumps . . . her and me on white sheets. We smoke cigarettes when we're done, blowing smoke rings in the air. I haven't smoked in thirty years but I might light one up if she wanted me to. Totally wrong for me, but I still have this fantasy that it could work out, that it could all work out. With the blonde and with Richard.

Got to stay focused here. I'm trying to pretend I'm in a therapist's office and that Richard the Tall is my therapist, when we're actually sitting outside in the back courtyard of Factor's and now it's hot as hell out here. We're under a huge umbrella—but my arm is outside the shade line and it's getting fried. I'm staring at the pickle bowl thinking I should have dressed hipper and not worn my Vans tennis shoes. Too casual for a power lunch. I'm thinking about what to say so I can save this situation and not lose this guy, but I'm not sure I want to get into a whole lot of detail about my life with my father. And now I'm starting to panic a little and I have to fight to stay in control.

"Look, Richard, here's the thing: There have been a lot of positives growing up the son of Leonard Nimoy and plenty of negatives. You have to understand that my father is first-generation American, born to Russian immigrant parents who had nothing when they arrived in Boston. During the Depression, when he was ten years old, my dad sold newspapers on the Boston Common in the dead of winter. When he came to L.A. to become an actor, without his parents' blessing or support, he worked a dozen odd jobs to provide for himself and later for his family. No one gave him anything: Every dollar in his pocket was his. I, on the other hand, was raised in sunny

Southern California and never really wanted for anything. When *I* was ten, *Star Trek* started airing, and in the years that followed, things became pretty comfortable in the Nimoy household. I never had a paper route, I had an allowance. I did well in school but didn't have to work my way through and maybe that was a mistake. When you have a generation gap like that, there's plenty of room for conflict. And it's taken a hell of a lot of work to bridge that gap, and sometimes we're successful and sometimes not.

"But I think it's important for you to also understand that I've spent my entire life struggling to create my own identity. That's one of the reasons I became an attorney until I finally realized that, for me, it was a dead end. So I'm not totally averse to getting into the *Star Trek* stuff and maybe some of the complications of being my father's son. But most of my writings revolve around my life today, in terms of my recent divorce, raising two teenagers, and dealing with recovery after thirty years of substance abuse."

Richard stops eating and just sits there in silence, looking down at his plate. I think he's going into some sort of shock. I mean, I can actually see his face going pale. Those dollar signs are definitely fading as he shifts in his seat, the blood draining from his face like he's about to be sick or something. He reminds me of that guy in *The Crying Game* when he discovers that the new love of his life is really a transsexual.

Richard clears his throat. Then he looks up at me through those black trendy, expensive glasses. His mouth starts to move.

"I didn't know you were a writer."

"I guess Scott didn't tell you. I mean, I have written a number of things about my life growing up and I'm absolutely willing to consider using some of that material. But I'd really like the emphasis to be on what's been going on over the last three years since I sobered up and moved out of my house."

More shifting in his seat and then he leans back like he's trying to catch his breath. There's some color returning to his face. Finally, he tells me to send him some of my work along with some of my *Life with Leonard* stories. And while Richard halfheartedly insists on paying the check, my mind is already racing about which stories from the past might be appropriate to use along with the more recent stuff I've been writing.

First my mom, then Scott, and now Richard. Everything comes in threes. Maybe I do have to start thinking about that growing-up crap.

The credit card is signed and the lunch is over. We get up to go. The blonde gives me one last going-over with eyes that tell me she's willing. I've been alone for months and I'd really like to sleep with her.

But then, of course, I'd have to kill myself in the morning.

BEGINNING OF THE END

WE HAD NEVER been to the Christmas Parade on Hollywood Boulevard. But in the winter of '65, we decided to see what it was all about. I was nine and my sister, Julie, was ten. Dad took us while Mom stayed at home. We got there late and the sidewalks were packed and we couldn't see anything, just the silhouettes of bodies blocking Hollywood Boulevard, which was all lit up. We walked up and down the block trying to find an opening but it was wall-to-wall people and no one would let us in. We each took turns as Dad put us on his shoulders so we could see which celebrities were being driven down the street, waving from convertibles. But we were too heavy and Dad couldn't hold us for very long. We decided to leave, and as we were walking away, Julie told Dad that next year we should come earlier and get a good seat. He agreed.

And we did go back the following year. Only this time, *we were in the parade.*

As we sat up on the back hood of the car smiling and waving to the crowd, a friend of mine from elementary school broke through the police line and ran up to our car to say hi. That was cool. But the funny thing about being in the parade was that, even though it was exciting, we *still* couldn't see the parade, only the lit-up faces of all the people who wouldn't let us in the year before.

The spring of '67 brought the annual carnival to St. Timothy's, a Catholic school at the corner of Pico and Beverly Glen. It was a weekend and Dad was willing to take me. I hadn't seen much of him since *Star Trek* started shooting the previous summer. The routine we were getting used to was that he would leave for the studio very early in the morning, come home to a late dinner, learn his lines for the next day, and then go to sleep. I was pretty used to Dad not being around. Even before *Star Trek*, he was off doing guest roles on dozens of TV shows or he was working the numerous odd jobs he had going on the side. And when he was home, he was often preoccupied with home-improvement projects. So I was pretty excited about the prospect of going with him to the carnival.

When we got to St. Timothy's, it was crowded. We went straight to one of the game booths, but within minutes some kids came up for autographs. Even with the Spock haircut brushed to the side, Dad was easily recognizable. At first, it was only a few kids, and I figured once he finished with them we could move on to the rides. But then the crowd started to grow until kids and their parents were swarming around him as I was being pushed away. Finally, Dad came over to me.

"Adam, we have to go."

EXACTLY WHERE I'M SUPPOSED TO BE

TODAY IS TUESDAY and I'm waking up in my sleeping bag on my air mattress in my new two-bedroom apartment off Venice Boulevard where the only furniture is my fold-out camping chair. Just last Sunday, I was sleeping in my bed in my big beautiful house in Cheviot Hills in West L.A. Now I'm staring at the ceiling, the white stucco ceiling of my apartment, trying to remember how the hell I got here.

I think it may have started when I began to lose my television directing career, due in no small part to my pot problem . . . and my bad attitude. The two kind of go together because I would stop smoking when I was directing, feeling that if I screwed something up, I didn't want it to be because I was stoned. What I didn't realize was that when I wasn't smoking, I was in constant withdrawal, which meant I wasn't sleeping well, which meant I was often irritable, which meant by the time I got to the set and started to make my way through a thirteen- to sixteen-hour day, the chances were pretty good that at some point I was going to snap at anyone who tried to mess with me. "They don't complain about the work, just the attitude," my agent used to say. It took years to build up that career and only months to kill it. "Nobody's gonna cry if you leave the business," my agent used to tell me. Nobody but me maybe.

And so, after thirty years of almost daily pot smoking, I

finally decided to sober up, which didn't do a thing for my directing career. What it did do was force me to face up to the fact that my marriage had been miserable for years, and it was time to get out. After eighteen and a half years and three failed attempts at marriage counseling with three separate therapists, I knew the day would come. And once I stopped drinking and using, I needed that day to come *now*. I mean, I knew we were in big trouble at the ten-year point, but the kids . . . Maddy was five and Jonah was three and I loved living in that house with those kids.

But now, even their crying and begging couldn't stop me and the guilt and the misery and blah, blah, blah, and do I have to think about all of that right now? There's plenty of time to think about it. Plenty.

White stucco ceiling and an empty apartment with white walls and white carpet that looks like it melted down during the last steam cleaning. I reassume the fetal position inside my sleeping bag and go back to sleep. That oughta make it all go away.

My cell phone rings. I recognize the number. It's Sub-Finder—the automated phone machine for the Santa Monica Malibu Unified School District, where I now work as a substitute teacher. In an attempt to make productive use of my time while I figure out what my next (read *third*) career might be, I became certified as a substitute teacher and I'm finally getting calls from the district. One of my first jobs was at the John Adams preschool, and I pray I don't have to go back there. I pray they're going to put me in the upper elementary grades or maybe the middle school or, even better, the high school. I mean, I know it was a lesson about humility and attitude: teaching the ABC's to little kids and then pushing them on swings. And I tried to do a good job, but I pray they put me in the upper levels.

I answer the phone. An automated voice comes on, the kind where it's the voice of a robot woman and there are pauses where a real human woman gives you the specific information.

"HELLO. THIS IS THE SUBFINDER SYSTEM. . . . The Santa Monica Malibu School District . . . HAS A JOB AVAILABLE. YOU WILL TEACH . . . kindergarten and first grade level. . . . THE JOB LOCATION IS . . . McKinley Elementary School. . . . REPORT FOR WORK AT . . . eight o'clock AM. . . . TO ACCEPT THIS JOB, PRESS 1. TO REJECT IT, PRESS 2. FOR MORE OPTIONS, PRESS 3."

I have to think about this for a second because this is just above the preschool level and I'm not sure I can handle it. I've got a law degree. I've directed some top network television shows. And now I'm being offered a job subbing at the kindergarten and first grade level. I really don't want to do this.

"TO ACCEPT THIS JOB, PRESS 1. TO REJECT IT, PRESS 2. FOR MORE OPTIONS, PRESS 3."

But I need the work and I know I should just bite the bullet and do it, so I go to press 1, but I press 2 by mistake.

"YOU HAVE REJECTED THIS JOB. THANK YOU FOR USING SUBFINDER. GOOD-BYE."

"No, Robot Woman! I made a mistake and punched the wrong number!"

I jump out of my sleeping bag and desperately call Sub-Finder to get the job back. After much pacing and maneuvering through the system, I finally press the right button and get the job. I flop back down onto my air mattress, which pops its cap, and I slowly sink to the floor.

———

Except for the occasional attitude mishap, I used to be a very good television director. It's not an easy job: The days are incredibly long and you're on your feet most of the time, struggling to shoot as much film as possible within the time allotted. You get tired and you get hungry. But when that camera is rolling and you're standing beside it, watching great performances being captured on film, all the pain and fatigue and hunger fade away. And you start to feel like this is where you were *meant* to be, this is where you *belong*, that all the events of your life have led you right up to this very moment, the moment when that camera is rolling and the actors are on their marks and everyone is waiting for you to say, *"Action!"*

But now it's 7:45 on a Tuesday morning, and I'm on my way to McKinley Elementary School to teach kindergarten and first grade.

I arrive at the main office fifteen minutes early and a nice Armenian woman gives me the keys to the classroom. I get to the class and the place is a mess: There are toys and books everywhere and the teacher's desk has mounds of paperwork. I start to wonder what I'm doing here. And then I remember something my dad once told me about directing TV: that even on the lesser shows, the rubbish I didn't want anyone to know about, something will happen—I'll learn something or I'll meet someone who will make the experience worthwhile. With that in mind, I read through the lesson plan I manage to find on the desk.

The kids line up on the playground as some of the parents smile and wish me luck. The bell rings and I lead the kids into the classroom. Some are troublemakers who have no interest in listening to directions. And there's a know-it-all girl who's

on top of everything and will someday make a fine U.S. senator. In the middle of the day, she raises her hand and informs
me I'm doing "a very good job." And there's a boy who comes
in late. His name is Seth. He has short, wild curly hair and
wears cool clothes: dark blue turtleneck shirt, faded jeans,
black shoe boots. His dad walks in behind him and doesn't
acknowledge me as he says good-bye to his son. The dad looks
like the funky-groovy-artist type: long hair, loose-fitting jeans,
weathered corduroy jacket with elbow patches. He kisses Seth
good-bye. In front of all the other kids, he kisses him. And
it's the type of display of affection that some people (like me)
might find a little too sentimental, and that others (like me)
might find somewhat embarrassing, and that still others (like
me) find essential for the proper functioning of this planet.

Seth plays beautifully with the other kids. When it comes
time for free play, he asks me to bring down a box filled with
hats and he puts on a fireman's hat and a yellow jacket and
totally immerses himself in the role. Then it comes time to
read individually. The kids walk over to the couch area to find
books. Seth walks up to me.

"I don't like reading time."

"What don't you like about it?"

"I don't get it. I can't understand the books."

"Well, okay, let's look at a book and see how you do."

I pick up a short book and sit next to him and he starts to
read. I go one-on-one with him and let the other kids fend
for themselves because if I were their regular teacher, I'd be
doing this with each of the kids throughout the school year.
Although Seth stumbles here and there and I have to correct
him, he makes his way through the pages. It's a well-written
story about a greedy snake that catches more than enough

field mice for his supper. One clever mouse outsmarts the snake, enabling all of them to escape. Seth and I get through the entire book, and when he's finished, he seems to feel a sense of accomplishment.

Then we go out to recess, and I watch them play on the field and the jungle gyms. Again I start to wonder what I'm doing here. When it's over, I lead the kids back to the class like a mother hen as they follow behind. While we're walking, Seth comes up to me and hangs on my arm as he skips along. It's as if he's telling me he trusts me, that I'm one of his pals. And that's when I finally get it, that's when it becomes clear to me that being at McKinley Elementary School on this particular Tuesday is exactly where I'm supposed to be.

RECIPE FOR AN ADDICT

I'M HANGING MY head out the back window of Dad's maroon Mercedes puking my guts out as he curves through the night down Sunset Boulevard. It's 1976 and I'm twenty and Dad's driving and Mom's in the front seat and Rae, my girlfriend at the time, is sitting next to me in the back. As Dad drives, I just keep puking all over the side of his beautiful 1970 280SE with the 4.5-liter engine. I'd hate to be in the car driving behind us. I'm probably splattering all over their windshield. And in between bouts, I keep thinking to myself, *How the hell did I get here? How . . . the hell . . . did I get here?*

———

How I got there is pretty simple really; in fact anyone can do it.

1. Start by smoking pot all day.
2. In the evening, go out to dinner at, say, a Japanese restaurant with your parents and your girlfriend or boyfriend.
3. If you're underage (like me), just ask a parental unit to order a large sake. Drink as much as possible before the waiter notices.
4. Order shrimp tempura and chicken teriyaki and eat all of it.
5. Go to a Hollywood party. (*My party of choice is at Bernie*

Taupin's house, Elton John's collaborator. Bernie and Dad met in London. I have pictures of them where Bernie's desperately trying to make the Vulcan salute.)

6. Upon arrival at Hollywood party, hobnob with some of your idols. (*At Bernie's, that would be Bernie, Alice Cooper, Steven Stills, and Dennis Wilson.*)

7. Act cool by ordering a glass of scotch on the rocks. Chivas Regal, if available. Johnny Walker will do. If not, any other hard liquor will substitute just fine.

8. Drink entire serving and allow to simmer with already ingested sake and half-digested shrimp tempura and chicken teriyaki.

9. Let stand for half an hour to forty-five minutes while you continue hobnobbing.

10. Feel fine. Feel numb. Feel something stirring in the pit of your stomach.

11. Tell girlfriend you have to go to the bathroom and that perhaps she should follow.

12. Enter bathroom and begin first round of puking your guts out.

13. Miss toilet bowl so girlfriend has to clean up after you.

14. Walk out through front door while girlfriend notifies your parents.

15. Walk through the flowerbeds to get to the sidewalk because you can't find the steps.

16. Ignore valet guys, who now watch your every move.

17. Pass out on the front lawn, spread-eagle.

18. Lie half-conscious until the rest of your party arrives.

19. Allow parental unit (Dad) and girlfriend to drag you into backseat of Mercedes 280SE or any other luxury automobile. (*Luxury automobile preferred for heightened dramatic effect when puked upon.*)

20. Have parental unit drive away and speed down curvy street like Sunset Boulevard.
21. Stick head out window.
22. Open mouth.
23. Begin puking.
24. Wake up next morning with dried puke in your hair. Take a shower. Feel much better.
25. The following weekend, repeat.
26. Wake up thirty years later. Take kids to school. Take shower. Eat breakfast. Reach for bong.
27. Repeat daily.

FIRST MEETING

I'M GOING TO an MA meeting for the first time. I found it on the Web for marijuanaholics. It's being held in a church not far from our first house on Palms Boulevard. My parents bought that house in the late fifties and Dad spent weekends fixing it up. It was for sale about ten years ago and I went inside to take a look. It was tiny. And it was run-down. Now the same yellow house with white trim sits totally dilapidated, as if no one's truly lived in it since we left in '62.

My kids and I are on the phone constantly because they miss me now that I don't live with them and they always want to know where I am. I don't want them to know about my drug problem, not yet anyway, so I tell them I'm going to an evening writing class.

I get to the meeting and it's weird. A bald guy "welcomes" me. He tells me to collect phone numbers, to start to get to know people. I look around the room: freaks and geeks whom I don't want to get to know. One guy's in a suit. Everyone else is in T-shirts and old jeans. These aren't my people. This can't be where I'm going to end up. Where are the attorneys? Where are all the Hollywood types? I know they're out there because I've heard about them and I used to work with them in law offices and on set.

I take a seat. The chairs are arranged in three semicircular rows that face each other. Across the room, I see a pretty girl with long dark hair. Really pretty in a sea of not-so-pretty.

They give out poker chips to newcomers who are in their first thirty days of sobriety. I stand up and take a chip because I want the girl with the long dark hair to notice me. Someone yells out, "How'd you do it?" I didn't know I was supposed to say anything and I debate how much of my story I should tell to this group of unattractive strangers. I decide to keep it simple. "I changed my living situation."

Other people take chips for sixty days, ninety days, and six months of sobriety. People get up and take their chips and hug Johnny, the chip person. Johnny's heavyset and scruffy-looking. At the end, when everyone has taken his or her chips, Johnny says, "Thank you for letting me be of service." The hugging part is pretty weird, like it's just a formality and no one really wants to hug Johnny, least of all me. Then they celebrate birthdays for continuous years of sobriety. Steve, the bald guy I met when I first came in, gets up to take a cake for twelve years of sobriety. We all sing "Happy Birthday," and at the end, instead of "And many mooooore . . ." the refrain is "Keep coming baaaaack . . ."

After the chips and the cake, a surfer dude named Jason sits at the head of the semicircles and talks for twenty minutes. He's very tan for the middle of winter and has greasy blond hair. He tells his story of what it was like to be a drug addict, how he sobered up, and what his life is like now. Very little of what he says is of any interest to me, so I just look at the girl with the long dark hair. Jason finishes and other people around the room get two minutes to share their hard-luck stories and how they found their lives again in "these rooms," which I figure is a euphemism for 12-Step meetings.

At the end of the meeting, the pretty girl announces she's

in charge of putting the room back in order and asks if anyone wants to help. Some people raise their hand, including me. When the meeting's over and she starts rearranging chairs, I walk up to her and ask what the rearrangement is supposed to look like. She puts out her hand and says, "Hi, I'm Lynn."

"Hi, Lynn, I'm Adam."

Lynn tells me what to do, and at that moment I'd do anything for her. I help rearrange the chairs, and when it's over, Lynn thanks me and I decide she alone is reason enough to come back to the meeting next week.

I return the following week but Lynn isn't there.

MY DOLLY

MY DAUGHTER, MADDY, still has the two dolls she carried with her everywhere when she was little. They're Madeline dolls from the famous books by Ludwig Bemelmans. Separate friends gave her the same doll because Maddy's full name is Madeleine. The Madeline dolls are very colorful: blue dress, white blouse, red hair, yellow hat. Maddy called them "Baby Hat" and "Baby Hair" because her favorite word was *baby* and because early on, Baby Hair lost her hat. She took them everywhere and she held them close. Sometimes she'd undress them and lay them out on the coffee table and try to put diapers on them.

When Maddy was nine and her brother, Jonah, was seven, we took them to Olvera Street, a Mexican marketplace located in the oldest section of Los Angeles. They loved the colorful booths of clothing and leather goods and glass sculpture and jewelry. We bought Jonah a sombrero and a set of maracas. We found a pretty dress for Maddy that was handwoven. It was a dark blue pullover with little birds woven into the hem. Maddy tried it on and we could tell it wouldn't fit for long, but it looked so pretty on her that we bought it anyway.

Then came December and the Hanukkah party at my mother's house and Maddy needed help getting dressed.

"Mom! Come downstairs and help me get dressed! I don't know what I'm wearing!!"

"Maddy, I'm getting dressed too so you'll just have to wait!"

I'm downstairs all ready to go, helping Jonah put on his dress shoes.

"I'll help you, Maddy."

"No, you don't have to, Daddy."

"But I want to."

I follow her into her room. Her windows face west and the setting sun comes streaming in.

"Dad, I just don't know what to wear. I don't have anything I like."

I look through her closet.

"How about this? The dress we bought you at Olvera Street. You've never even worn it."

Maddy brightens. "Oh, yeah."

She puts on a white, long-sleeved turtleneck, then pulls the dress over her head, and it's just long enough to still fit. She steps into white panty hose while I pull her red clogs out of the closet. She looks so colorful, just like her Madeline dolls, and I hold her and squeeze her just like she used to hold and squeeze Baby Hat and Baby Hair.

But by now, Maddy's outgrown those dolls. Now they sit high up on top of her bookcase looking down on us. The Madeline dolls are worn. Baby Hat is missing a stitched eye and Baby Hair doesn't have hair anymore.

And I can't help but wonder, when was it that Maddy put her babies away and became a big girl. When was that moment, that exact moment, when she had me put her babies high up on the shelf never to be taken down again? Did we know then that would be it for Baby Hat and Baby Hair?

I can hear the parrots coming. The wild parrots in our neighborhood that screech and squawk as they fly this way and that in their groups of twenty or so. I read that some parrot owners discovered that they make terrible pets and released them from their cages. They fly high overhead in the late afternoon, free against the sparse clouds that litter the deep-blue sky.

And now Maddy's fourteen. And she's mad at me—really mad. She refuses to even visit me at my apartment, so every morning I pick the kids up from the house and take them to school so that I can see them. Tonight, I come home from the MA meeting and there's an e-mail from Maddy waiting for me.

"Dad, I hate you so much. I never want to see you again. EVER! I hate you, I hate you, I HATE YOU!"

On Monday, I pick her up from school. I know she doesn't eat breakfast and she has only a cookie at snack time, and at lunch she's too busy talking with her friends. So by the time I pick her up, she's starving, and when she's starving there's a good chance there's going to be trouble. So I always bring a cold pack filled with food. Today it's half a turkey sandwich, string cheese, carrots, chips, and a drink. And she eats everything while I drive her home.

I come back later to help her with her math homework—graphing quadrilateral equations, which I learn from the text and then teach to Maddy. It's a routine we've been through many times before. And Baby Hat and Baby Hair sit high up on Maddy's shelf watching us. And by the end of the night, as I get ready to leave to go back to my apartment, it's "Thank you, Daddy. I love you."

On Tuesday, it's Spanish and I make flash cards of the vocabulary words and by the end of the evening, as I get ready to go, it's "Thank you, Daddy. I love you." On Wednesday, it's a Civil War book jacket and why two days of bloodshed at Shiloh might have been a turning point in the war. And on Friday, it's *To Kill a Mockingbird* and how Atticus killed a rabid dog in a symbolic attempt to take on the racism running through Maycomb County. And again, as I kiss her good-bye, it's "I love you, Daddy" while the Madeline babies sit in silence and watch over us.

THE LIVED EXPERIENCE

WHEN I STILL lived at the house, most Sundays were spent working in the vegetable garden. One Sunday, I'm out there digging and planting when Jonah appears.

"Dad, can we go to the music store to buy some new drum-sticks?"

Jonah's eleven now and he's been playing drums since he was eight. I know a few songs on guitar. And every so often, at any given moment, he'll come up to me and say, "Dad, can we play a song?"

And if I have the time, I always say yes because it's fun jam-ming with him.

But today, he needs a new pair of drumsticks. He shows me his old pair and they're all chewed up. I tell him the only drum shops open on Sunday are in Hollywood and that I'll take him if he feeds the fish and cleans out the lizard's cage.

When he finishes the chores, I go inside to get ready and I tell him that we have to visit Sylvia and Orky after we get the drumsticks. He nods and says okay, like he's totally willing to come with me to visit my eighty-four-year-old cousins.

We drive to Guitar Center and park on a side street. And as we walk down Sunset Boulevard, on another picture-perfect day in L.A., I remind him that he's probably one of the best eleven-year-old drummers in town, and the best part about that is that he's in my band. He turns to me and says I'm one of the best forty-six-year-old guitar players in town, and the best part about that is that I'm in *his* band. That's when I hold him and squeeze him and kiss him.

At this point, we've been jamming together for almost four years, and so far we pretty much have the same taste in music.

Basically, I've brainwashed him on '60s and '70s tunes. Then he found my copy of Nirvana's *Nevermind*, and now our repertoire is full of Kurt compositions. But I've never taken him to Guitar Center because I know he's going to want to buy everything in the place. And when we walk into the main display room, there are hundreds of guitars hanging on the walls from floor to ceiling. Jonah sees other guys playing the guitars and he insists I take one down for him. And of course he sounds great, even though he's only recently started to play.

Four guitars later and I have to tell him this is the last one. Finally, we walk upstairs to Drum Heaven, where they have about a dozen drum kits all set up with people banging away. Now I'm sorry I didn't bring my earplugs. Jonah gets some sticks and starts playing on one drum set after another. And now that I hear him play on a full-sized kit, it confirms what I've known for a long time: This kid knows what he's doing. He tells me he needs a new snare. I agree and tell him to start saving.

I finally drag him off the drums and we buy a set of drumsticks, and we manage to get out of there having spent only $6.50. I take him to In-N-Out, his personal favorite, for a delicious, unhealthy burger, and then we stop at RadioShack for some telephone batteries.

That's when the trouble starts.

They have this big display for remote-controlled cars and he starts in about how he *needs* one. I remind him he has four or five of these things at home, but he tells me they're all broken. I say that I'll check them out and see if I can fix them when we get home, but he becomes more insistent and upset because he can't have a new one *right now*. We get back in the car, and now he's really pissed off. I try to pet his head, but he won't let me. And then I just leave him alone. I let him just sit there and think about it and cool down and live the experience. Oftentimes, I don't want to live the experience. Oftentimes, when things get difficult, I don't want to feel anything or deal with anything or experience anything. I just want to numb myself. That's why I'm a pothead.

That's not the life I want for him.

The real problem, Jonah tells me, is that he doesn't want to go to Sylvia and Orky's. Now, I know it's hard to drag an eleven-year-old boy on a Sunday afternoon over to some old farts' apartment. But it has to be done and he agreed to go with me. And I tell Jonah that Orky's my oldest friend and we need to visit him because he won't be around much longer. I remind him how much Orky's been through in his life, how he lost his entire family in a fire when he was eight and the only reason he survived was because his father lay down on top of him.

I stop talking as we drive down Jefferson Boulevard.

Jonah calms down and goes along with it without a word. Soon enough, he lets me pet his head. And he's very sweet while we're visiting the old and gray and shrinking Sylvia and Orky, and they are so happy to see us, even for just a short time. When we leave, he feels good. I can tell he *knows* he did something very right.

When we get home, we go into the garage that we've converted into a little studio. He gets behind his mini drum set with his new sticks. I put in my earplugs and pick up my guitar. Something comes into my head, a chord progression, and I start strumming fast and he starts drumming fast and he's right there with me and pretty soon we're wailing on something that sounds like surf-music-meets-punk-rock. He watches me and he picks up all the changes I throw at him and we get really tight on this as we wail away.

That's when I start thinking to myself: *Nobody has what we have. Nobody.* But that was last year.

Tonight, Jonah's angry that I'm not there anymore to put him to bed. He claims I promised I'd be around to put him to bed, and I explain that I can't do it when his mom's there. I tell him I can put him to bed at my place if he would just come over, that I miss doing that and that if he could just come over for the night sometime, I could put him to bed. But he keeps saying that's never going to happen. And then Nancy, their mom and my ex, comes home because I've been hanging out with them for the evening while she was out. And I say good night to Jonah and tell him I love him.

"I wish I could believe that," he tells me.

Then he says he's mad at me because I won't come home for him, that I don't love him enough to come home. And it just kills me, but there's nothing I can do now because Nancy's home and I really need to go. Everything's cordial between us although there are occasional flare-ups. We gave couples therapy one more shot after I moved out, but it just led to more yelling so we stopped going.

I say good night to Maddy and I'm out the front door and lock the top lock from the outside. I get in my car and drive back to my apartment. I pull into my designated parking spot and just sit there.

That's the real beauty of being sober: You have nowhere to go, no place to escape to, and nowhere to hide. Instead, you get to feel the pain. You get to live the experience.

SPACE-MAN/SPIDER-MAN

IT'S MOTHER'S DAY 2001, three years before I would sober up and move out of my house. We're taking my mother to brunch in Westwood. We're going to the Moustache Café. Everyone seems to be enjoying themselves: my sister's family, my family, and my mother. I bought my mom a turquoise bracelet, and my wife, Nancy, gave her one of her illustrations, which she had framed, and it looks really terrific. The card I give my mom is one of those flowery things, the kind with the fancy lettering that goes on and on about how she has always been there for me, how she's always cared for me and supported me, how she'll always be a very important part of my life. I hate these kinds of cards but she loves them and so every year I buy her one. This year, I can't resist, so I sign it, "You're adoring and loving son, Frank." When she sees that, she laughs. Thank God she sees the humor. And she hands it to my sister and Nancy, who also get a kick out of it.

Across the dining room, in the bar, the Lakers game is on TV. I try to watch it, but I can barely make out what's going on though I know they're behind. We finish the meal and the chocolate soufflés. My mother signs for the check and absolutely no one feels guilty about that. Then we all kiss and hug and leave.

Nancy and the kids and I are driving back to the house when, on a whim, I decide to pass through my old neighborhood where we lived after we moved out of the house on Palms Boulevard. As we drive down Beverly Glen, I make a left on LaGrange. I always feel a chill when I come up to the top of LaGrange because that's where I rode on the back of John Wall's motor scooter in 1964, with the wind blowing in my face and a brand-new song playing in my head called "All My Loving."

We make a right on Comstock and drive down to my old house. It's still the same. A pretty Spanish-style home, only now it has lots of trees and shade in front. It looks good. It feels good.

I remember running up the steps to the front door: It was the mid '60s and I had a *TV Guide* in my hand. I bought it at the Food Giant, now the Ralph's, on Olympic Boulevard. I was so excited to show it to my mother and my sister because it had an ad for a new TV series about a cool-looking crew on a spaceship exploring the far reaches of the universe.

I remember the bags of mail that started coming to our house on Comstock Avenue, the fan mail that started coming by truckloads in the spring of 1967 after *16 Magazine* accidentally printed our home address in one of their issues.

At first, getting all that fan mail was great. But the fun soon wore off when the whole family had to answer the letters by stuffing envelopes with autographed pictures. Around that time, I ordered a Spider-Man T-shirt and a pair of those X-Ray glasses that were always being advertised in Marvel Comics, the ads that promised that with the X-Ray glasses, you could actually see through a girl's clothes. Every time the mail truck arrived, I thought, *Maybe today. Maybe today I'll finally get that Spider-Man T-shirt or I'll get to see all those naked girls.*

Week after week, the sacks of mail kept coming. But the

letters and packages were always for him. Finally, the T-shirt and the glasses arrived. The shirt was a size too small, and I couldn't see a thing through the X-Ray glasses.

And the packages kept coming.

For him.

———

I see a man gardening out in front of my old house. I pull into the driveway and introduce myself and the family. He says he's Don, the guy who bought the place from my parents back in '68. The boxes crammed floor to ceiling in his open garage leave no doubt that this guy's been living here for almost forty years. He's really happy to see me, tells me some of the changes he's made to the place, mostly restoring things on our pretty white stucco house. He tells me the brick wall my father built along the driveway had to come down and that some fans came by and wanted to buy a brick. I get a good laugh out of that. So many rabid fans out there. Then again, if Ishi had built that wall, if the lone survivor of the Yahi tribe had touched those bricks, then I'd probably want one too. The kids want to take a look inside, but Don begs off, telling us his wife isn't there and the place needs tidying up. I'm not that anxious to go in anyway. As we say our good-byes, Don tells me that he found some pictures of my dad in the house and that he'll e-mail them to me.

The next morning, I find three pictures in my e-mail, pictures I've never seen before. They're publicity photos, and suddenly I'm looking through a time portal that takes me back to 1966. The first picture is of Dad with his hair glued to his head, his bangs cut straight across, his eyebrows half shaved. He's sitting at the wooden chess table in our living room considering his next move. Across from him sits my mother, also apparently pondering her next move, even though she never played chess.

The second picture is of Dad sitting on the steps between the dining room and the living room holding Brunsie, our dachshund, who's trying to lick his face. The third is a picture of my father sitting in front of our pretty white house. You can see the whole bright front of the house clearly because back then, there were no trees. My father has a big smile on his face and that space-age hairdo. Sitting in the bright sunlight of the 1960s on top of a brand-new world that started with that *TV Guide*.

The phone rings, putting an end to my walk down memory lane. It's my mother. Mom's a great gal with a big heart. But she's also a Jewish mother, and I should have seen it coming:

"Why did you have to ruin my Mother's Day by making a joke out of that card?"

HAPPINESS IS BIRD WINGS

IT'S STILL WINTER, the winter I moved out of my house, winter in L.A., which means that any day we'll be having a heat wave. But tonight it's cold. It's 10:40 PM and I'm sitting in my car in front of the skating rink. Just like she told me. 10:40 PM when the rink closes. Maddy says good-bye to her friends and gets in the car, and she's really happy.

"Dad, I just met the coolest guy. His name is James and he is *so* cute. I just can't believe I met him and I think he likes me."

She's so happy to tell me, and I'm so happy to hear this, because the kids have been really angry and upset the past few weeks about the fact that I don't live at home anymore.

Maddy is so excited that it reminds me of the time she was in preschool and she was in love—with her class and her teacher and with Matthew. One day, I walked her into school and she said I didn't have to walk her into class and she ran into class so happy that she lifted her hands and flapped them up and down really fast with her arms close to her sides, like a little bird flapping its wings. And now, ten years later, she's sitting in my car and she feels so good that she wants to share it with me.

His name is James.

Weeks go by, and because James goes to another school, I don't hear much about him. This weekend I'm driving Maddy all over the place: to Nia's house and Jamie's and Erin's and

Sarah's. Nimoy's Taxi Service. She sits in my car and her little phone keeps ringing and she has to talk and coordinate with all these girls, and sometimes, she has to deal with catfights.

"Maddy, you're just so popular. How do you handle it?"

"I like being popular, but sometimes I can't deal with it. It gets so complicated and too much work and I just can't handle it when people get into fights."

The girls are all going to a boy's house today. Maddy and Sarah and Nia are going to visit James. It takes me a while to even remember that it's James from the skating rink. He lives in Culver City. She's very excited, and although they're not boyfriend and girlfriend, she tells me they are such a good-looking couple. I figure I must be doing something right for a teenage girl to tell this to her dad, a dad who doesn't live at home anymore, a dad who still, occasionally, gets hell for it. I'm so relieved to think I must still be doing something right.

"What does his father do?"

"I have no clue."

"What about his mother?"

"They're divorced."

When we get there, the neighborhood is a little funky but the house looks okay. There's an old Lincoln Continental and an even older Chevy Malibu sitting in the driveway. The other girls are already there, standing at the front door waiting for Maddy.

"Should I come in and meet James's father?"

"No, Dad, it's okay."

"Maddy, I think I should come in and check it out."

"Dad, no! None of the other parents did that and you don't need to come in. Love you. Bye."

And she slams the door and runs off all excited just like the day she ran into her preschool class, hands flapping.

I drive away.

And as I head down Overland Avenue, I start thinking about all the things I need to do to get my career back on track. I'm thinking about the brain cancer fund-raiser I'm working on and about the rabbi I've been interviewing, the rabbi who had a brain tumor that miraculously turned out to be benign. I'm thinking about something he said when he was first diagnosed: that he wasn't so much afraid for himself as for his wife and especially his seven-year-old daughter. He said he was terrified when confronted with the possibility of his daughter's future without him. And that gets me thinking about Maddy. Then I start thinking about that old Lincoln and the Chevy Malibu sitting in the driveway. Then I get this feeling that something's wrong. And then it hits me:

Dude, wake up and get with the program! You just dropped your daughter off at some stranger's house. Remember when you were her age and you found yourself in the wrong place at the wrong time doing the wrong thing because no one was watching?

I make a U-turn.

Right in front of a cop.

But the cop doesn't come after me. I race back to the house. I jump out of my car and ring the doorbell. The dad answers. Holy shit.

"Hi. I'm Adam, Maddy's dad, and I just wanted to say hello and introduce myself."

The dad's got short gray hair, thick silver hoops in both pierced ears, a snaggletooth among his front teeth, and deep lines in his face. He reminds me of Keith Richards, like he's done some serious partying, like he's been to hell and back via the mainline. He has this sour look on his face like I interrupted him when he was in the middle of doing something.

Like slamming heroin.

"Hi, I'm Chris, James's dad."

With some trepidation, I offer my hand.

"Yeah, hi. Yeah, I just dropped Maddy off and thought I would come back and just say hello."

"Sure, no problem."

And then there's this awkward silence while I think about how the hell I'm going to get her out of there. Or maybe I should just sit in my car out front in case she needs me. Or maybe I should call the cops and do a background check on Chris. But I'm looking at Chris, I'm looking at him, and I start thinking he sort of looks familiar. There's something about him that reminds me of someone and it's not Keith Richards. And then I suddenly figure it out; it's the snaggletooth.

"Chris, what's your last name?"

"Kelton."

"Kelton? Chris Kelton? Oh, my God, it's me, man, Adam Nimoy!" Chris's eyes go wide. He breaks into a smile, giving that snaggletooth center stage.

"Adam Nimoy! No way!" He opens his arms for a bear hug. Then he invites me inside.

When I was in high school, Chris was best friends with Matthew, my next-door neighbor, and the two of them taught me just about everything I ever needed to know about drinking and getting high. One of my favorite memories is of Chris standing in my bedroom, and he's got this huge head of curly black hair and he's wailing away on a Stratocaster guitar that's plugged into a waist-high amplifier I was borrowing. And of course, we were wasted. Chris and Matthew were a year older than me and I just thought they were so cool. Needless to say, my parents weren't thrilled about our beautiful relationship.

But Chris is sober now and has been for twelve years. We sit and talk for almost an hour about our trials and our sobriety and how we're going to deal with our kids and drugs.

James comes out of his room, taking a break from his harem. Chris introduces us. James is tall with dark wavy hair and a cute face, the kind that makes it easy to imagine what he must have looked like as a boy. He goes to the kitchen for a glass of water then back to his room. Chris and I continue our conversation about people we know and what they're doing now and about how he managed to put together twelve years of sobriety after horrible struggles with heroin. Chris tells me he hit bottom so hard that at one point he got down on his knees and begged God to either kill him or show him the way. That's when he found Alcoholics Anonymous.

Maddy appears. Apparently, James just told her I was sitting at the dining room table with Chris.

"Dad, what are you doing here?"

"Honey, Chris and I were friends when I was growing up in Westwood."

She sort of pretends to get mad and acts like she wants me to leave. But I know that inside, she's happy. Happy to have me around. Happy to know that I cared enough to come back. Happy that I'm friends with James's dad, which gives her a leg up on the other girls—who are also into James—because it puts the focus back on her.

When we finally leave, I give Chris a big bear hug good-bye and promise to go to an AA meeting with him. By now, the MA meetings have gotten a little dull. Especially because Lynn with the long dark hair is rarely there anymore.

I drive Maddy back to the house.

"Dad, I saw you hugging Chris good-bye. Why did you do that?"

"Because Chris is like a long lost brother to me, honey, and finding him was incredibly lucky and made me really happy. And it's all because of you."

And then I squeeze her knee. I do this all the time, I reach over and gently squeeze her left knee, and with intensity I say, "You've got knees, Maddy. You've got the knees in the family!"

We drive down Palms Boulevard. Along the way, we pass by that first house my parents bought.

Still dilapidated.

THE LISA SCHWARTZ
SCHOOL OF DATING

IT'S BEEN MONTHS now and the kids still won't come over. Sometimes I lie in bed and just ache to have them near me. We've finally managed to find a therapist the kids and I both trust, and the therapist tells me that because he's twelve and she's fourteen, this is a hard age to get them to do anything because they're old enough to make their own decisions. I'm just going to have to be patient.

"Things will get better." That's what Paula tells me. Paula's in my writing class. She's recently divorced with two kids, was in AA back in New York, and has been sober for years.

"In a year's time, Adam, things will be so completely different you won't even recognize yourself. I promise you."

Paula is smart and pretty. T-shirts and jeans, Frye boots, blond, petite. I talk to her on the phone all the time. But when I try to ask her out, she reminds me that she has very young children and that she's just not ready to get involved. She always puts me off, but she always welcomes the phone calls. Maybe it's too soon for me too. But I'm not like Paula, because she's got primary custody of her kids. And I'm starting to think there must be some separated or divorced moms out there who *would be willing* to at least meet for coffee. Because let's face it, cyber girls are helpful, but they're not available for coffee and they certainly can't keep you warm in bed at night.

My friend Lisa says I'm a great candidate for Internet dating because I've had the experience of a long-term marriage, so I'm clearly not afraid of commitment. The fact that I've managed to keep most of my hair and some of my girlish figure is also a plus. She gives me some hip singles Web sites to check out and then she gives me some pointers, the Lisa Schwartz dating tips:

First, she tells me that women lie because they post old photographs of themselves and that I should trust her on this because she's done it many times herself.

Next, she tells me to meet these women right away, that I shouldn't exchange too many e-mails with them or talk too much on the phone because people can seem very clever and then turn out to be very disappointing when you meet them in person.

Then, you have to meet them for coffee, not for lunch, not for dinner—just coffee. You don't want to spend a lot of money on someone you may never want to see again.

Finally, you can meet for only forty-five minutes max. You have to say you have to be somewhere in forty-five minutes to pick up the kids or pick up the cleaning or walk the dog, because within the first minute, you're going to know if there's an attraction, and within the first five to ten minutes, you're going to know if there's an agreeable personality. And even if there *is* something there, you've got to give yourself an out to take a breather and not ruin it.

And then you can call for that second date.

So that night, I start casually looking at Internet dating sites, and I freak out because I discover that several of my ex's single girlfriends are plastered all over those sites, and if they ever saw my picture, I'd never hear the end of it and I'm just not ready for that.

Then Michael, a buddy of mine, says he wants to fix me up with a woman he met at the gym. He assures me that Terry is pretty and has a great figure and might be perfect for me. Michael e-mails me what he says is a recent picture and he's right: Terry is a knockout. I'm also happy to learn that she's Jewish. And her résumé looks exactly like someone I'm looking for: about my age, divorced with two grown kids, a good job, lives close by, grew up on my side of town. Having graduated from the Lisa Schwartz School of Dating, I make a date with her right away. But I don't quite follow the Schwartz Protocol, where first dates are only for coffee, because without even thinking about it, I find myself asking Terry to dinner. *(Sound of warning buzzer.)* But, hey, this is different: I didn't meet her over the Internet, and she came highly recommended, and I'm in love with her photo, which Michael tells me is recent, so I figure it's probably okay to bypass this one rule. *(Second warning buzzer.)*

I pick Terry up in front of her condo and she is gorgeous, with beautiful long brown hair. I bring her red roses, and she says she likes me right away because of the roses. It all looks so good, so incredibly good.

During the short ride to the restaurant, I learn that Terry's father has all but abandoned her. As I make a left on 26th Street, I learn that her mother is a chronic gambler. As we drive down Main Street, she informs me that she doesn't get along with her brother and that she resents her sister-in-law. As I park near the restaurant, I'm told that her ex-husband is a total loser.

As per Rule 4 of the Schwartz method, within the first ten minutes, I realize there is no way in the world this is ever going to work out.

At our table, I learn that Terry lived alone with her brother while in high school. Her dad was living with his third wife and her mother was working on the East Coast. After graduating, she fell in with some spiritual group in Phoenix and one of the leaders seduced her. Ten years later, she woke up and realized she was the mother of two boys and married to an abusive husband and absentee father and that she had to get the hell out. She made it to L.A. on her own and her wealthy father would help only by paying moving expenses. She's supported herself for the past five years by working in the clothing industry and she's in with a *new* spiritual group whose credo is to express gratitude each and every day for all the things God has given us in life. But Terry has so much resentment it seems like the spirituality thing is just not working. And she tells me her kids are giving her a hard time because she has nothing nice to say about their father. And when I finally get to speak and tell her how I deal with my daughter when *she* gives *me* a hard time, Terry tells me I'm much too lenient and I have to be tougher if I want to see any change in her behavior.

While she keeps talking, I start wondering if I can just turn this into a physical thing. What if I can base this relationship on sex? But once the sex was over, I'd be thinking about getting the hell out of there, and exactly how long is appropriate to wait after doing it before it's okay to get up and go? Twenty minutes? Thirty minutes? I'm so new to this I just don't know. Note to myself: Must ask Lisa Schwartz about this. But the way Terry's going, I'm not sure I could last five minutes. And then I start to hate myself for even thinking of sleeping with her, and I just keep listening and nodding as she keeps talking. And the evening drags on . . . and it's getting hot in here . . . and this restaurant is so damn noisy . . . and where the hell's that waiter with the check . . . and holy shit, it's ninety dollars! And when

I finally get her home, I shake her hand and call her "Carrie" and feel terrible as I stumble through my apology.

The next day, I tell Michael what happened and he tells me that Terry is reluctant to go out with me again because I'm not divorced. He says he argued with her because that didn't stop her from going out with this dentist who was abusive, and he assured her that I didn't fit into that category.

"Michael, no! You don't have to convince her to go out with me again. I'm happy to have the decision not to move forward be hers."

Note to myself: Must remember to meet them for coffee—not dinner, not lunch, just coffee. And I have only forty-five minutes, I need to leave in forty-five minutes, because I have a soufflé in the oven or I'm flying to Fiji or I have to give my cat a medicated bath. Even if I like them, just keep it to forty-five. Because they lie. People lie. Their pictures lie, even if they do look that good in real life.

THE HALLS ARE HELL

IT'S MY ANNIVERSARY today. It would have been nineteen years. Since I'm not divorced yet, I guess *it is* nineteen years. Although things are beginning to normalize between us, I don't call Nancy to celebrate. I'm pretty much set on moving ahead with the divorce, but Nancy's in no big hurry and the therapists all say to take my time and let the kids continue to adjust to not having me around all the time. So in honor of my anniversary, I decide to show up to a new semester at writing class.

I like the class because you have to bring in material and read it to everyone, and it forces you to do the work and it allows you to get feedback. I need that more than ever now because without the weed, I'm having trouble sitting down to do the writing. That's one of the other side effects of living without pot: You no longer have that immediate urge after taking a hit to sit down at the typewriter and write every little thing that comes into your stoned head, and before you know it, you've been writing for two hours straight. And in the morning, in the sober light of day, you reread the material and keep the stuff that sounds interesting and throw out the stuff that's really crap that you probably wouldn't have written if you weren't so high. So I need the class to force me to write down all the stuff that's happened to me. All the incredibly wonderful, miserable things that have happened since I put down the weed and the booze and moved out of my house and into my apartment off Venice Boulevard, the apartment my kids absolutely hate.

I also like going to writing class because on any given day, there's usually about fifteen women in there, and only three or four guys. I go to the first meeting of this session of the class. A couple of guys and a dozen or so women, some of whom I know from previous classes, including Paula, who looks just so damn pretty in her white T-shirt, corduroys, and boots. But there's a new guy there named Justin. I'm not really happy about him because he's younger and good-looking and I don't like having competition. Mid-thirtiess, long dark hair, black Dickies pants, black Converse tennis shoes, no socks. I make a mental note to keep an eye on him, maybe even hoping he washes out.

Even though it's the first class, I'm ready to go with fresh material I managed to crank out at one AM without the weed. I get up and read "We Have Our Man," a story about how I was hassled by the Isla Vista Foot Patrol when I was a student at UC Santa Barbara in 1975 for allegedly stealing hashish from some knuckleheads I was trying to rent an apartment from. The whole idea of those jerk-offs complaining to the police that I stole their hash was something I thought amusing enough to write about. And apparently so does the class because they're laughing through much of it, which makes me feel good.

But Justin one-ups me: He gets up and reads this story about the various ways he would fake prescriptions to get opiates from the pharmacy to feed his habit. He'd do things like imper-sonate doctors over the phone, and he's impersonating these doctors during the reading and it's funny as hell. Especially the Russian doctor. I really want to hate this guy for crashing the class, but I can't stop laughing.

At the end of the class, Jack, our fearless leader, passes out a class list with all our personal information. And then he goes around the room as people tell him they want to change their address information or their phone number or their e-mail address. This goes on for about five minutes until finally, Justin raises his hand.

"Jack, I'd like to change my name."

Justin's a recovering junkie who's been sober for four years and he takes me to some pretty cool AA meetings. I like hanging with him because he's a good writer, he's funny, and he plays a mean bass, both stand-up jazz and electric rock 'n' roll.

He takes me to a Monday night meeting in Mar Vista and it feels good to be there. It feels comfortable. And one night, there's a big turnover in commitments. They're reassigning jobs like setup and cleanup and making the coffee and bringing AA literature, and Justin urges me to take a commitment. And so I opt for the literature commitment, because I figure it'll get me to read more of the material. And when I get the assignment, he turns to me.

"Now you're sure to get laid."

"Really?"

"Works every time."

I still like Paula from my writing class. But she still won't date me. It doesn't really matter because we talk all the time in class and on the phone. We talk about single parenting and about sobriety, she having also been in the program when she lived in New York.

"You're not in the program at all anymore?"

"I'm still sober, but now I attend Al-Anon meetings. Twelve-Step and therapy and astrology. I've done it all and it all works on some level. It just depends on where I'm at in my life."

And I would tell her what's been going on with me and she'd say things that made so much sense. She'd tell me little slogans she learned from AA in New York that helped her get through the early days of her own sobriety, things like "The halls are hell," meaning that transitioning from one point in your life to another can be brutal. And "Feelings are not facts"—that just because you feel something doesn't necessarily mean it's true. And one of my personal favorites, "Don't just do something, sit there!"—you don't have to react to other people's craziness when it's directed at you because often it's not really about you anyway. It's because there's something else going on and they just happen to be taking it out on you. This is something I've known for some time and have occasionally been clearheaded enough to put into practice.

When I was fourteen, my family spent some time in Spain, where Dad was in a western called *Catlow* starring Yul Brynner and Richard Crenna. A seriously flawed movie, *Catlow* looked like it should have been made for TV. Dad played Miller, the heavy, and he really looked the part with his black beard, buckskin jacket, and custom-made rifle. Miller was the leader of a pack of young, hip bad guys with long hair and ponchos and the grit and grime that came with the trail. When I was on the set watching them shoot, it was perfectly clear to me that Miller was the coolest character in the movie.

At first we stayed at Hotel Aguadulce, which was on the Costa del Sol, but after a few weeks, Dad rented us a house nearby. There were a number of problems with the house and it was some distance from the beach.

One night, we were all having dinner back at the hotel. Dad

was agitated and having a heated discussion with Mom about the situation with the house. Mom and Julie and I wanted to move back to the hotel, but Dad wasn't happy about the costs involved in staying at the hotel and argued that the house was just a short drive to the ocean. In a lame attempt to lighten the proceedings, I casually mentioned that the Mediterranean is not an ocean, it's a sea. He lit into me.

"Don't smart-mouth me!"

There was much more, although I can't remember the words. But I can still see his mouth moving as he continued to unload. I was stunned and embarrassed and sorry that I opened my mouth. He remained angry with me for the rest of the night. And even though I felt a tremendous sense of guilt, for the first time, at fourteen and a half, I realized that this wasn't just about me. Besides the house, there were issues with the movie, problems on the set, personality clashes or creative differences that I didn't fully understand. Then there was the fact that Dad himself repeatedly admitted that he was, is, and probably always will be a tough kid from the tenement streets of Boston. And when he feels threatened or undermined, his impulse is to come out swinging.

The next morning, I went to Dad to show him a cane my mother bought for me when we were in the nearby city of Almeria. The handle of the cane was carved in the shape of a dog's head. When Dad woke up, I sat on his bed and told him the story of the dog's head cane, how it once belonged to a wealthy Spanish nobleman who died years ago. The cane was sold off to an antique store and sat there until I happened along and found it hiding in the back behind some furniture. Dad said that was a good story and everything seemed to be okay again.

Ultimately, we moved back to the hotel.

I really want to spend more time with Paula. She tells me that sometimes she goes out to the movies alone and I suggest that we could go alone together.

But she just won't budge.

One day, she came to class and she looked nicer than usual. She was wearing makeup for the first time and, though feelings may not be facts, and I may be your typical it's-all-about-me addict, it sure as hell felt as if it *was* about me. I came in late and sat some distance from her and I couldn't take my eyes off her while she sat behind Andy as he read his piece. Andy's an excellent writer and I had to keep looking down at the ground to concentrate on what he was saying because every time I looked up at him and saw Paula, I couldn't concentrate. All I could think about was her face and hair and the white jeans and the tie-dyed T-shirt and she's looking at me now and I'm looking at her and . . . doesn't she feel *anything*? Maybe I'm just obsessing because I used to obsess about weed all the time—where to get it, how to smoke it, when to smoke it—and I don't have those thoughts raging through my head anymore and I have to obsess about something. And all addicts want what they want right now, at least this one does.

I finally break away from her gaze and look back down at the ground and Andy's voice becomes comprehensible to me again.

I go to the house to babysit the kids while Nancy is out. It still feels weird being there, but I'm glad to be with the kids. This is one of the biggest benefits of getting along with Nancy—there's no big issue about my coming over to see them. I help Maddy with her homework and feed her apple slices while we're working. Then I go into Jonah's room when he's ready for bed, and I read him some Bible stories. He's really tired and falls asleep right away.

I go back into Maddy's room and help her put away some clothes because her room is a mess since her mother decided to repaint it. It looks good. The part that's finished anyway.

She tells me she wants to sleep in Jonah's room on the futon. I say okay but we have to pull it out without waking him. We finally get a sheet down and a blanket and I grab a pillow from her room. She gets in under the covers. I lie down next to her, put my arm around her, and whisper in her ear as she's turned away from me.

"I love you so much, Maddy. You are the best daughter I could have ever asked for."

"I love you too, Daddy. I just wish you'd come home." And then she starts to cry.

"I know, honey, but I can't and I am so sorry. I am so, so sorry." I hold her close and hug her tight and then start talking to her about other things.

"Daddy, will you help me put the rest of my room back together on Tuesday when I have the time?"

"Of course. I would be happy to. Good night, honey."

"Good night, Daddy, I love you. Are all the doors locked?"

"Yes, sweetie, all the doors are locked. I love you too."

Nancy finally comes home and I head out the door, hating the fact that she gets to stay with them and I don't.

I get in my car and drive back to my apartment. I pull into my parking spot in the garage and, again, I just sit in self-doubt, wondering if I made the right decision or if I totally screwed up my life.

The halls are hell all right. The halls are hell.

DON'T CALL ON ME

SO I GO to the Friday night meeting at the Culver Center. I don't usually go to the Culver Center because there are always old-timer alcoholics there who have missing teeth and weird hair. But Chris Kelton, James's dad, is the treasurer on Friday nights, so I go to hang out with him, and sometimes we get dinner afterward.

This is a speaker's meeting, where an invited guest stands at the podium and talks about his or her experience before and after getting into the program. This goes on for about twenty minutes and then it's tag sharing, where people share their experiences, usually starting with something the speaker said that got them thinking. I don't really like tag sharing because I seem to get tagged when I really don't have anything to say, and when I do think of something, I don't get tagged.

Sometimes the speakers are really funny, like the guy who used to stay at home and drink all day and had mini palm trees and heat lamps set up in his living room so that he could feel like he went somewhere without ever leaving the house. Sometimes the speakers tell really tragic stories, like the women whose lives were so out of control they lost custody of their children. They cry as they tell these stories. Even though they've been reunited with their kids and they've probably told this story at a million meetings, they still cry.

When I put myself in their position and think of what it might have been like to lose my own kids, it just kills me.

The speaker tonight is a woman in her forties and she's not particularly funny or tragic. Then it's time for people at the meeting to share. There are about fifty people at this meeting and there's usually time for about ten shares around the room. It's pretty much the usual, where people thank the speaker and then talk about something the speaker said, or they talk about whatever the hell comes into their head. Sometimes it gets pretty painful. Chris is tagged, and because he's the treasurer, he's sitting up in the front of the room facing the crowd, and he's saying something about his own experience, but I'm not really listening because now I'm worried Chris is going to call on me and I gotta think up something to say. And I'm trying to hide behind the people in front of me so that Chris doesn't see me, so there's no eye contact, so he knows to please go ahead and call on someone else. And then he finishes his share and the next thing I hear is, "Adam, would you care to share?"

I AM SOMEBODY

IT'S SEVERAL MONTHS later and now I'm Mr. Everywhere in the Santa Monica Malibu Unified School District substituting for math, science, English, and social studies teachers at all the grade schools. Teaching at the middle and high school level can be a tedious babysitting job with hormone-raging kids, but on some days, things happen. On some days, there's a really great lesson plan that I can get excited about and I go from class to class trying to get the kids as turned on by the material as I am. It almost feels like the days when I went from directing one television show to another—when I went from *NYPD Blue* to *The Practice* to *Ally McBeal* to *Gilmore Girls*. I was hot. I was living in the fast lane. I was somebody.

When Jonah was a toddler, he'd stand in his crib in the morning and yell at the top of his lungs for someone to wake up and come get him. And Marta, our eighty-year-old Romanian refugee babysitter would always tell us when he yelled from his crib, "He vants you shuud know 'I am somebody! I am somebody!' He vants you shuud know."

We all just vant to be somebody.

Jonah's going to be somebody. He's bound for rock 'n' roll glory. I should know, after having my ears blown out from more than forty years of concert experiences. I was sitting in his room the other day, listening to my twelve-year-old wailing away on his electric guitar. This is the way it's been going lately; some days he's mad at me and things are rough, and some days I'm hanging out with him just like I used to and everything's fine. Right now I'm watching him rip through yet another Jimmy Page solo, and I swear this kid is on fire.

Now, if I can just get him through school and keep him out of rehab, I'll have done my job.

────────

It's six-thirty the next morning and I'm lying on my new IKEA bed. I have some furniture now. It's nice to have furniture that you can put together yourself with simple tools that come in the box. IKEA gives the furniture funny Swedish names, like Malm for the dresser and Yagurt for the lamp and Sven for the bed and Yarnahorst for the dining room table and chairs. I'm lying on Sven recounting all the reasons I left my house and kids, thinking about all the things that led to the breakdown of my marriage: all the neglect and the conflict and the counseling and the fights and the misunderstandings and the miscommunications and the missed opportunities and the extended family issues and the financial issues and the drinking and the smoking and the . . .

My cell phone rings.

It's SubFinder. Robot Woman needs me.

"HELLO. THIS IS THE SUBFINDER SYSTEM. . . . The Santa Monica Malibu School District . . . HAS A JOB AVAILABLE. YOU WILL TEACH . . . seventh grade science, middle school level. . . . THE JOB LOCATION IS . . . John Adams Middle School. . . . REPORT FOR WORK AT . . . eight o'clock AM. . . . TO ACCEPT THIS JOB, PRESS 1. TO REJECT IT, PRESS 2. FOR MORE OPTIONS, PRESS 3."

I have to think about this for a second because I don't know a damn thing about seventh grade science.

"TO ACCEPT THIS JOB, PRESS 1. TO REJECT IT, PRESS 2. FOR MORE OPTIONS, PRESS 3."

I really need the work, so I press 1 and roll out of Sven and into the shower.

I like subbing at John Adams because Maddy's in the eighth grade there, and I get to see her because those kids simply will not come to my place. When I arrive, I'm told I'll be teaching sixth grade social studies for periods one through three, then it's over to seventh grade science. I walk to the social studies class and quickly read the lesson plan. It's Janet Baker's class and she's pretty thorough with her lesson plans. I know most of the kids in her classes and some of them are really rowdy. They're studying Mesopotamia and Egypt, so I run over to the library and check out a huge book with some great photos of statues of the heavyweights from Mesopotamia and a book about Egyptian mummies.

After announcements and attendance, and just before Aaron and Omar and Wiley can start making trouble, I tell everyone I have some pictures to show them about the stuff they've been studying. I open the book on Mesopotamia, hold it high over my head, and in a deep, booming voice announce: "I give you Nebuchadnezzar, king of Assyria." And I slowly pan the picture across the room. I turn the page. "I give you Hammurabi. I give you GILGAMESH!" The kids sit gawking at these incredibly heavy dudes. And when we move on to Egypt, I show them pictures of all those mummified kings who were unwrapped. I show them Imhotep and tell them I think this guy looks pretty damn good for a three-thousand-year-old man with no cosmetic surgery. I show them Ramses and tell them this guy built great cities and had dozens of kids and scientists believe he probably died from an infection brought on by a bad tooth because he didn't brush regularly. Complete silence in the room. Even the troublemakers sit in awe. This kind of thing works only for so long before we have to follow the lesson plan and the kids actually have to do some work, and that's when all hell breaks loose.

At lunch, I walk across campus to get myself a slice of pizza. Because I'm a teacher, I get to cut in front of the line. After the pizza, I head over to the science bungalows when I see Maddy and her eighth grade friends standing around talking. Proof certain that she doesn't eat during lunch, she just talks and talks, which is why I bring a cold pack full of food for the ride home. Because feeding Maddy will reduce my chances of a meltdown by about 50 percent. Maddy's with Becca and Sarah and Alexa and Jamie and the Paris twins, Robbie and Charlie. The Paris brothers are straight-A students and they're famous for switching clothes in the middle of the day and going to each other's classes just to mess with their teachers. They turn to me and wave and yell out, "Hi, Mr. Nimoy!" They're enthusiastic because I've had them in class and they think I'm a good sub. But I still can't quite tell them apart, even when they don't switch clothes. Maddy just turns away and pretends not to notice me. I know she's a little embarrassed that I work there. I know she's still mad at me for moving out. But I also know she likes having me close by.

I head over to Karla Delian's room in the science bungalows. I write my name on the board as kids start coming in. One of the Latino boys comes up to me and asks if I'm related to Leonard Nimoy. I can't believe this kid's into *Star Trek*. He's too young.

"How do you know who Leonard Nimoy is?"

"I watch him on *The Simpsons*."

I've never heard that one before. I mean, I know Dad did some stints on *The Simpsons,* but this was the first time anyone told me they knew him exclusively from that show. I'm starting to feel old.

Then he says, "Are you his brother?"

————

The students are supposed to design a space suit for an astronaut going to Mars. We have to read a fact sheet about the planet so that they can design a space suit to deal with the environment. And the temperature can get to a couple of hundred degrees below zero on Mars and there's no atmosphere to keep out the sun's harmful rays and there's no oxygen or water. I try to get some energy going because everyone's totally lethargic after lunch. And now that I think about it, it's the same way on the set: In the morning we're jamming to get as many scenes done as possible, but after lunch it's like the whole production goes into slow motion. And it's the director's job to keep the energy going. So I turn it on.

"What about eating? How's this guy going to eat? There's no Mickey D's on Mars. There's no In-N-Out Burgers. He's got to carry his own food and water. Where you going to put all that stuff on his suit? This is the kind of thing you guys have to think about. And how's he going to get to it? How's he going to get to his food and how's he gonna stick it in his mouth? Forget about eating, what if he just has to scratch his nose? How's he gonna do it?"

The students are bored. Usually, enthusiasm is infectious, whether it's on the set or in the classroom, but right now it doesn't seem to be working. We're in this huge room that looks like it could have been a car mechanic's garage. The windows are high up and it's just walls everywhere and it's dark because the kids don't want the overhead fluorescents on. Caleb, the kid in the front row, has a Mohawk and wears a green army jacket and jackboots. And I happen to know his mother drives a beat-up Cadillac with a horrible black paint job that looks like the family got together for a bonding experience and spray-painted the car. I like Caleb because he pays attention.

"Have you ever had a nose itch and for some reason you couldn't scratch it because you have, like, mud on your hands? It's pure torture. But can our astronaut just pull up his visor and stick in his glove and give it a little scratch?"

Someone manages a no.

"No! But tell me why? Why? Somebody tell me why. Why can't he just flip up his visor? Why, why, why?"

Caleb opens his mouth. "Because of the sun?"

"BECAUSE OF THE SUN! BECAUSE THERE'S NO ATMO-SPHERE ON MARS TO BLOCK OUT THE ULTRAVIOLET LIGHT AND IF HE FLIPS UP HIS VISOR, HE'LL FRY HIS FACE OFF!!"

A few of them are watching now.

"And what if he has to go to the bathroom? I mean, do you think he can just walk behind some Martian rocks and whip it out?"

This gets them going. The girls start giggling. Someone gives me a no that has a little punch to it.

"No! And why not? *Why not?* Why, why, why?"

One of the Latino kids raises his hand.

"Because he'll get burned?"

"Exactly! He can't just stand around and whip it out because HE'LL FRY HIS DICK OFF!!!"

That *really* gets their attention. There's murmuring now among the boys and some of the girls are outright laughing.

And then I realize I just said "dick" and I wonder if that's going to put an end to my new career as a substitute teacher, the short history of which now flashes before my eyes.

But the students are finally pumped. They actually pick up their pencils and start to draw what this space suit should look like. And some of those drawings are detailed and creative. Some of them are very colorful, in contrast to the drab white suits NASA likes to produce year after year. So I figure, what the hell. Whatever it takes to get these kids going. Even if it costs me my job. Even if it costs me my new career.

Because right then and there, in Karla Delian's seventh grade science class, it feels like I am somebody.

MR. TOAD AND SPIDEY

IN 1968, WE moved into our third house, a beautiful home in Westwood. During that period, Dad would work on *Star Trek* during the week and then spend weekends making personal appearances all over the country. I went with him on a few of these excursions. He would get up in front of a crowd and play the three or four chords he knew on guitar and sing songs. As a kid, it amazed me that he was able to get up in front of so many people and perform like that.

After one of the trips he took alone, he came into my room and gave me a present. I opened a small cellophane-wrapped package and inside was a set of Mr. Toad cuff links and a tie clip. I knew right away that it was a gift for a seven- or eight-year-old boy. I was twelve. But because he thought of buying me something while he was away for no particular occasion, the Mr. Toad set became a prized possession.

After I turned thirteen the following summer, I kept the Mr. Toad cuff links and tie clip in one of several jewelry boxes I had been given as Bar Mitzvah presents. I kept them with other treasures, like my first watch—a broken Timex—and all the other cuff links and tie clips I received as a Bar Mitzvah boy. Years later, the Mr. Toad cuff links and tie clip disappeared along with a blue star sapphire ring that had belonged to my grandfather. I'm pretty sure the star sapphire ring was lifted, but I don't know why anyone would have wanted the Mr. Toad cuff links. Anyone other than me.

In the early '60's, when we still lived on Comstock, I started collecting comic books. Mostly DC Comics in those days, like Batman, Superman, The Flash, and Green Lantern. During the summer of '66, I was in Pico Drug, an old-style drugstore with an ancient soda fountain and the best shoestring French fries ever. It was close to where my grandparents lived, so I would walk over and check out the comic book situation. And there on the rack was a cover that would change my life. It was Spider-Man #27, *Bring Back My Goblin to Me!*, and it showed Spidey in chains being hassled by a ring of bad guys while the Green Goblin looked on. What a cool cover! How had I missed the first twenty-six issues of this amazing superhero?

Between 1968 and 1971, during the middle and end of *Trek,* I attended Emerson Junior High School. In art class, Kurt Hammond, this cool, long-haired troublemaker, would refer to me simply as "Ears." At any given moment, he would call to me from across the room, "Hey, Ears!" just for a laugh. It was kind of nice to be considered worthy of the attention of one of the cool kids. Even if he was a screw-up.

I became friends with a kid whose older brother worked at the Cherokee bookstore in Hollywood. Upstairs, hidden in the back of Cherokee, was the comic book department, and this hippie-type guy had put together floor-to-ceiling boxes of collectible comics for sale. My dad took me there a few times to buy some. My friend's brother offered to sell me the #1 Spidey for fifteen dollars. That was a lot of money back then, but I pulled it out of my Bar Mitzvah fund and bought it.

I still have a collection of comics hiding in a footlocker, and I never sold a single issue. Except the #1 Spidey. Two years after I bought it, I sold it for thirty dollars. My father congratulated me on making 100-percent profit. But I spent the thirty dollars on things like french fries at Pico Drug and hot fudge sundaes at Kirk Drug on Westwood Boulevard.

In the early '70s, Dad started getting into photography. He set up a little studio in the garage, and one morning he dragged me out of bed to sit for pictures, which I totally resented because I hadn't showered and my hair was squished on one side of my head. A picture from that sitting still hangs in my mother's house. He also happened to take a picture of me with that #1 Spidey. In it, I'm sitting on my bed with a tray table looking at some of the comics in my collection and there, in a plastic bag, is the #1 Spidey. To this day, the picture still haunts me because selling that comic was one of the biggest mistakes of my life. Depending on the condition, it now could be worth more than $100,000.

But the real tragedy wasn't selling the Spidey. It was the loss of the Mr. Toad cuff links.

ONE STEP FORWARD

THE SCHOOL YEAR ended and Maddy graduated from middle school with honors. She became a counselor in training at the day camp at the Cheviot Hills Recreation Center. She got to take care of the little kids. She loves little kids. And she loves her twelve-year-old brother.

One day, when he was home alone, Jonah called me because he wanted something to do or someone to be with him and I told him Maddy might have to go home early from camp because she wasn't feeling well. And sure enough, when I went to drop off her lunch, she wanted to go home. And when she walked through the front door, Jonah was there and they hugged each other and didn't let go. I felt left out.

"Don't *I* get a hug?"

Jonah came over and gave me a little slap in the face and we all laughed as I grabbed him and then grabbed her and held them and squeezed them, and, oh my God, this could turn out to be okay.

TWO STEPS BACK

"ADAM, NEXT YEAR things will be different. Things will be so totally different that you won't even recognize yourself."

That's what Paula told me only a few months ago, but right now, that's pretty hard to believe.

Last night Maddy and Jonah came over for dinner. It's been months and months and they finally came over. They were standing in my living room and Maddy cried, and then he cried, and then they both cried. Then they begged me to come home and I had to just sit there as they begged me. They *begged* me. Jonah told me how lonely he is for me to be with him and to put him to bed at night and to wake him up in the morning. How am I supposed to respond to this? I'm constantly going through the litany in my mind, reminding myself of all the signs and all the things that happened through the years that made it perfectly clear to me that my marriage was over. It's a nice long list and it's in my hard drive and I cling to it now. But the litany is not something I care to share with my children. Instead, I tried to tell them how bad I feel, and that I understand how they must feel, and that I'm lonely for them too. Both of them. But I just can't come back.

Maddy can't stand my apartment. She can't believe I could possibly want to live here in a two-bedroom apartment off Venice Boulevard. And she peeks into their room with the made-up beds like it's some sort of torture chamber. She tells me on the way over that room better be shut because she doesn't want to see it, and then when she does look, she can't believe that I bought sheets and comforters for the two beds.

And then Jonah admits he's crying because she's crying and I just sit there and take it and I start to think I could stop it and make them so happy *if I just came home.*

But then I think about what it would be like, and then, yet again, I have to go through the checklist in my mind of why I moved out and I realize there is no way I'm going back to that because there was never any indication that any of the problems were ever going to change.

But the kids. *What about the kids?*

They don't want to eat dinner because they lost their appetites even though Jonah goes into the fridge and pulls out a piece of cheese. And I offer to take them to dinner instead of cooking and they say okay—as long as Mom comes along. Maddy and Jonah are supposed to be having dinner with me, just the three of us, which is what they do with Nancy at the house every night while I eat alone. But Maddy changes her mind and calls Nancy to come pick them up and I say I'll take them home.

On the drive to the house, she keeps pushing.

"How can you do this to me? I'm through with you, Dad. How do you feel about never seeing me again? I will never, ever come back to your stupid apartment. How do you think it will feel to live alone for the rest of your life?"

I'm driving down Palms Boulevard past my old, trashed house trying to control myself while my hands grip the steering wheel.

"Well, Dad? How do you think it's going to feel? Dad? Are you going to answer me? Answer me, Dad. How's it going to feel?!!"

She's at full force. I should have fed her. And then she grabs the steering wheel and we swerve on the road.

"Maddy, let go!"

I pry her hand off the wheel and immediately pull over to the side and turn off the engine.

"That is so not okay and we're not going anywhere until you apologize. You could have gotten us into an accident."

"Well, what about my feelings, Dad? Did you ever think of that? Why don't you answer me? Don't just sit there, Dad. Answer me!"

And I'm at a total fucking loss as to what to do with her yelling, and Jonah's in the backseat yelling at Maddy to calm down. I'm totally lost and my mind goes haywire for a second because all I can hear is the sound of things crashing all around me.

We were living on Comstock. I was maybe six or seven. I was in the kitchen with my mother. Dad came in to fix himself a drink. It was in the afternoon and he made himself a martini and he put some lemon peel in it. Mom was looking for something in the refrigerator. Dad finished making his drink then shuffled off to their bedroom, leaving the bottles and the lemon and the knife on the counter. My mother pulled a bottle of milk out of the refrigerator. She lifted it over her head, yelled my father's name, and threw the bottle at the countertop. The countertop was made of tile. Avocado green. The bottle shattered and the milk splashed and a small piece of glass hit my brow. I ran out of the kitchen and into the living room. I hid under the coffee table, whimpering.

My father came into the living room and sat silently in a chair. He just sat there and said nothing.

———————

"Dad! Don't just sit there, answer me! Well, Dad? How's it going to feel? *How's it going to feel to be living the rest of your life alone in that apartment?*"

RENAISSANCE MAN

BEFORE *STAR TREK*, Dad had bit parts on dozens of TV shows. In between those shows, he juggled a half dozen part-time jobs. Between 1966 and 1971, he worked five straight television seasons: three with *Star Trek* and two with *Mission: Impossible*. When *Mission* was over, Dad started spending more time at home. But you can't stop a workaholic.

When we lived in Mar Vista and then later in West L.A., Dad always had some home improvement project going, whether it was building a patio, putting up brick walls, or landscaping the front yard. But when we moved to Westwood in 1968, he usually paid to have the work done and turned his attention to some of his many other interests. It was around this time that he started mixing colorful glazes for my mother's pottery. He started to delve deeper into photography. At the Westwood house, there was a small room behind my bedroom that was actually built as a darkroom in the '50s for the previous owner who was a portrait photographer. My bed was up against the common wall and Dad would be back there all night processing and printing and I'd fall asleep to the sound of him repeatedly pushing the button on the timer for the enlarger. It was also around this time that Dad was learning to fly single-propeller planes, which his parents were just "thrilled" about.

Being a Renaissance man, Dad pursued a number of other

interests, some of them slightly out of the ordinary. One of the things he did to fill his spare time was to paint a series of bricks. He painted red, white, and blue American flags on them, and next to the flags he wrote slogans like "My Country Wrong . . . Or Wrong!" This was during the Vietnam era, and in 1972, Dad campaigned heavily for George McGovern.

My mother still lives in the Westwood house, and last summer during a pool party, I was turning up the pool heater that sits behind the studio out back, and sticking out from a mound of dirt was one of those bricks. Though more than thirty years old, the paint was still pristine and it had the signature American flag and the slogan "Love It or Heave It."

I showed it to my sister and we speculated what it might fetch on eBay.

Dad also had a green thumb. He was always shuffling around in the garden tending to his azaleas, camellias, and fuchsias. In the studio, he built a mini hothouse. He built the frame and supports so that it stood at waist level, then he wired it to heat the soil and installed hoop supports for a plastic top to maintain the humidity. And then he started growing asparagus ferns, first from cuttings, then from seeds. It was his little science project, his little botany project: The Botany Bay.

One afternoon, when he was out there tending these plants, I was by the pool and he called me into the studio. I must have been sixteen or seventeen at the time. He was always calling me, summoning me. In the house, he'd call me from his upstairs bedroom, "Adam!" "What?" I'd yell back. And then there'd be this silence while I waited for his response, but it would never come, and I knew I had no choice but to go. I knew he was usually calling because he needed me to do something or he wanted to inquire about something like his missing tools, which I had a habit of borrowing and then forgetting to put back.

When I walked into the studio, he pulled some potted ferns out of the hothouse.

"Look at this. I grew this from a cutting—and this one I grew from a seed."

He was so proud of the plants, which I thought a little odd because, I mean, come on, they're asparagus ferns, which are very nice but not terribly remarkable, like, say, orchids. It was dark in the studio as the last light of day came filtering in through the windows behind his little hothouse. Dad was in the bathrobe and slippers he liked to wear when he was puttering around the house. I knew the ferns were important so I told him how great it was that he was able to grow the seedlings. But sometimes, I just couldn't control myself.

"Dad, you do realize you're not on the *Enterprise* anymore, right?"

COUNTY LINE

I USED TO daydream about camping at Leo Carillo State Park, which is a beach campground an hour's drive north of L.A. In my mind, I could see myself at this canyon camp full of trees just a short walk from the beach. And I finally figured out how to do it. I take Jonah and his friend Harrison so that we can camp and swim. We arrive in the afternoon, and after setting up camp, we walk to the beach. The boys bring their boogie boards, but Leo Carillo is very rocky and it's really a surfer's beach and there's no place for them to swim. I ask the lifeguard where we should go so the boys can catch some waves and he says County Line, which is five minutes north. On the spur of the moment, Chris, Harrison's dad, drives up from L.A. and meets us. County Line is a beautiful beach. We park on the bluff overlooking the water. There are surfers in black wet suits everywhere. The lifeguard says it's okay to boogie board as long as we stay out of the way. We ride wave after wave in the cold, clear water.

That night, the boys ride skateboards while I cook dinner: shish kabobs and roasted potatoes on my portable grill. We eat everything. After dinner, we make a fire and roast marshmallows and make s'mores.

The next morning, we drive back to County Line, and the boogie boarding is even better than the day before. I rest on my board in the chilly, clean water and the sun makes everything so blue and fresh and new. The kelp beds keep growing everywhere, a foot of growth a day they say, and a school of dolphins swims close by. When we finally come out of the water, I open up the towel that's wrapped around me and take Jonah in and hold him close to warm him up, his lips are so blue. And he makes fart sounds by blowing on my shoulder as I lean down to hold him.

After lunch, I just lie on the beach and watch him catch wave after wave on his boogie board. Mostly just white-water rides because the waves are so big. But he seems so happy.

Then Chris and Harrison have to go to meet up with the rest of their family. After we say our good-byes, Jonah suddenly wants to leave. We're in no hurry and I planned to stay and swim with him for another hour, but all of a sudden he's in a big hurry to follow them out of there. He's so insistent I finally agree, and as I start to pack things up, he lets me have it.

"I just want you to know I'm not having a Bar Mitzvah, and if I do, you won't be there."

"Why are you talking about this now?"

"Because I want you to remember."

"The minute they leave you have to jump on me?"

"Do you want me to do it when they're around?" And then he starts to cry. "Why did you leave, Dad? We had such a good family and then you just left. Why couldn't you sleep out back in the studio? Why did you leave me with Mom and Maddy? Just tell me."

"I know how you feel Jonah and I am so sorry. I am *so very sorry*."

"No, you don't know how I feel because it never happened to you! Why'd you do it, Dad? Just tell me."

And he's standing in his rash guard, the black swimming shirt I gave him that was mine but he needed it so I gave it to him. He's standing there, and the tears keep falling down his face as he stands there with his red cheeks and his wet hair, against the blue ocean and the white water and the kelp beds that keep growing. It's so painful to see him standing there crying after we had such a nice time.

I'm pretty sure Maddy and Jonah never saw it coming. I stopped arguing with Nancy in front of the kids a long time ago. After all the marriage counseling that went nowhere, there didn't seem to be any point to arguing. And when I became angry or frustrated, I would go off and smoke myself into oblivion.

"I know you miss me and I feel terrible about it, just terrible. Sometimes I think you got it the worst because you're the only boy there now."

"Then why won't you come back for me? *Please, Dad, just for me.*"

"I can't, Jonah. I just can't come back. I just can't. Let me hold you."

"No!"

And he just stands there and cries in his rash guard. And his red and blue Hawaiian flower swimming trunks. And his wet hair and the tears and the ocean is really pounding now.

"And why, Dad, why? Why did you leave me? Why? Just tell me why."

"There are a lot of reasons. Too many to try and explain right now. But I am so sorry. And I miss you too, Jonah. And I want to be with you."

"And you promised you would be at the house every day. You promised me and sometimes I don't see you and what am I supposed to do?"

And in that moment, I become so confused I actually try

to figure out a way to make it work, to come home if only just for him.

But that's crazy, because this is the hard part, where sometimes, at times like this, I can't quite remember the why, why, why. I've done so much work in AA, I've done so much work in my recovery and learning to let go of all the little injustices that happened to me during the course of my marriage is a big part of it. The letting go is such a big part of it and I'm beginning to forget the why, why, why.

But that's where everything gets screwy because to fight the vortex, to struggle against the kids who keep pulling at my heartstrings to come home, I have to hold on to some of that stuff, some of those injustices to remember why I left in the first place. Otherwise I simply don't have the guts to follow through on what I told myself I had to do. I have to remember about all the troubles and the neglect and the indifference and the love gone cold and all the counseling sessions that went nowhere. Nowhere with Hannah, nowhere with Carol, nowhere with Patricia. Absolutely nowhere.

It was just an hour ago when I sat on the beach watching him on his boogie board. When I sat on the sand and it was windy and I was watching him ride the white water. And he came in with the surf again and again, flopping around on his board, just like a little fish. He'd look up at me after a great ride, and I'd give him the thumbs-up, and he was so happy—happy to be in the water and happy to know I was watching. I'm sure he was happy. I'm positive. Or was it a dream?

And last night, when we were in our sleeping bags in the tent, I turned to Jonah and put my hand on his round face, the face with the almond-shaped eyes and all that hair.

"And when we get back to L.A. you'll go to kung fu without any problems?"

"Yes, I want to go."

"And you'll go to your guitar lesson?"

"Definitely. And I have to read my books, Dad. My two books before school starts."

But that was last night.

Jonah and I climb up the bluff and pack up the car to go home. He's still mad and upset and wants me to stop at a gift shop at Zuma Beach. After a three-day vacation on the coast that cost me all of fifty dollars, I'm more than happy to buy him some trinkets.

The place is full of junk but all he wants is a bar of soap shaped like a seashell. And after the gift shop, and then the market to get him a snack, he immediately feels better. And as we drive down the coast, he looks out his side window at the ocean.

"Thanks for this weekend, Dad. It was really good."

"Yeah, you're welcome, honey. It *was* really good. I think we did a good job and next time it's going to be better because I'll be better prepared. And we're going to have wet suits to protect us from the cold so we can stay in the water longer. Just like the surfers. Yeah, we're going to get wet suits."

PERMIT ME

THE SUMMER IS FADING. Today, I'm driving to the house to pick up Maddy and take her to register for her sophomore year at Santa Monica High. Afterward, we have an appointment at the orthopedist's because she's been complaining that her foot is hurting, the one she broke last year in a soccer game. So I pick her up and she looks really pretty because they take new ID pictures at enrollment. And I tell her how nice she looks, and she's all excited to reenroll in school and tells me she can't wait to start school again, that she's had enough of summer. She says she has all her paperwork and there are some things I have to sign. I look at the paperwork and I see that my address is nowhere to be found on any of the information cards we're supposed to turn in.

"Maddy, why don't you also put *my* address on the cards?"

"Because I don't live with you, Dad, and my home is at the house."

"Maddy, I'm hoping there's going to be a time when you *do* come to stay with me, and in the meantime, I would like to be on the mailing list for stuff coming from the school."

"Dad, I'm not going to be living with you because I live with Mom. And I'm not going to put the address of your stupid apartment on the information cards."

She says this as we're about to get on the freeway to Santa Monica. Maddy just sits there looking all determined in her pretty clothes and makeup. It's another clear and sunny day in L.A., which doesn't seem to go with this little storm that's brewing inside me. She's clutching the registration packet in her hand as she looks out the window.

"You know, Maddy, that is so unfair and really makes me feel bad. I do all this running around for you and get you to school on time and make doctors' appointments and get you to the math tutor and I don't get any of the benefits of having you with me. I mean, this deal of only seeing you when we're in the car is not very satisfying and I'm thinking that maybe Mom should drive you to school a few days a week 'cause I'm getting tired of showing up at seven AM on the dot just to shuttle you. I just want you to know that it really makes me feel bad not only that you don't come to stay with me but that you act like I don't even exist enough to put me on the registration information."

"I'm sorry, but that's just the way I feel right now. I mean, maybe we can work on it, but my home is at the house and that's the address I'm giving the school."

So, whatever, I give up. For now.

I get her to registration on time, early in fact, and we're way ahead of a huge line that's forming behind us and running right out the doors of the attendance office. All her friends are there, they're back from summer, and Maddy's so happy to be registering with them. They're all passing us by, on the way to the back of the line, telling us how smart we were to get there early. When we get up to the front and hand in the paperwork, the woman behind the counter looks at the address cards.

"So you're permitting in from out of the district?"

"Yeah, my mom has her office in Santa Monica."

"Do you have the permit from the district office?"

Maddy turns to me with a worried look. The woman behind the counter is a lifer—the type who's been here for years:

patriotic white blouse and blue sweater. A big woman, because she's been sitting at a desk for the last twenty years. She's very nice and tries to be patient as I look up at her.

"Isn't the permit on file from last year?"

"We have to have a new permit from the district office each year she enrolls. We sent a notice to your home during the summer about permit renewals."

I turn to Maddy.

"Well, I didn't know anything about this."

"Mom was online last night renewing her business permit with Santa Monica."

The woman interrupts. "But you're still going to have to go to the district office to get a transfer permit because otherwise, I can't enroll you."

There is no way I'm going to hold up the line arguing about this.

"Oh, okay, thank you."

And so, we walk away.

By now, I am so angry I can't even see straight. And I have to make a conscious AA effort to keep my cool before I totally lose it. We walk out of the attendance office past all those girlfriends who are smiling and waving and standing in line to enroll.

"You see, Maddy, if I had received that notice in the mail this wouldn't be happening. You know I would never have let this happen."

"I know, Dad. What are we going to do?"

I start walking quickly back to the car and Maddy follows. It's a huge campus and we have a ways to go, past Barnum Hall and the Technology building, to get to the parking lot. I love the SAMOHI campus. Even though it still has some decrepit parts to it, it's a nice campus with a good vibe. Today the weather's nice and sunny, and there's a clean breeze coming in off the ocean. But all that doesn't really matter right now as I pull out my car keys and pick up the pace.

"Dad! What are we going to do?"

"We're going to run to the district office and I'm going to beg them to give us a permit. But this really makes me mad."

"If I can't register today, I won't get to take my picture."

"I know, honey. Let's just hurry. We have an hour before registration closes. As it is, I have to call Dr. Grogan's office and cancel your appointment for your foot and see when we can get back in."

So I call the doctor's office as we're walking and rebook the appointment. We jump in the car and pull out of the parking lot, but everything's jammed at the front entrance because so many cars are trying to get in for registration.

"Dad, I just can't believe this is happening."

"Honey, if I had known that permit was required, we wouldn't be in this situation right now."

"I know, Dad. You do take very good care of me."

"I've always tried to take good care of you, Maddy. Always."

And I'll be damned if she didn't pull those registration cards out of her backpack right then and there and fill in my address.

IT'S MILLER TIME

"DAD, CAN YOU film me surfing?"

"Jonah, I really don't have time for that right now."

Jonah's learning to surf and he's been going pretty regularly with some of his friends from school. He likes it when I bring the video camera to get clips of him riding the little waves.

"Please, Dad. The surf should be really good. We'll just go out to Bay Street."

"I have a lot of stuff to do and I really can't be watching you for half an hour."

"Just for ten minutes, Dad. Come on."

"Yeah, well, it's never just for ten minutes, but I'll film you for fifteen."

It's a little windy and the surf's not that great but it's such a clear blue day and there aren't many people around. It's like my own private white sandy beach in the cool high noon of spring. I notice another guy standing farther up the beach. It's Dave Sanders, and he's also watching his son surf. Our boys go to the same school, and when they finally see each other out in the water, they hang out together waiting for waves. I walk over to Dave. He's been managing a restaurant on the Westside for years. I ask the usual small-talk questions: about business, how much longer he thinks he'll stay in the game, if any problem celebs ever come in and make a scene and have to be thrown out.

He starts telling me about Jason McCallum, the adopted son of Jill Ireland and stepson of Charles Bronson. He says that in the eighties, Jason would come in at ten in the morning and order lobster and two bottles of Dom Perignon for breakfast. Jill wrote a book called *Life Lines* about her attempts to help Jason battle his drug and alcohol problems, but Jason OD'd in 1989. I still think of him from time to time because although I was never heavily into narcotics, I often felt the pull. And I used to know Jason when he was a kid.

Charles Bronson died in 2003. He was eighty-one. Charlie happened to be in Spain shooting a film the same time Dad was there shooting *Catlow*, the western with Yul Brynner. At the time, I didn't know that much about Charlie. He was a big star in Europe but not well known in the United States. His breakout role in *Death Wish* was still three years away. But in 1971, he was in Spain making a western, *The Red Sun,* with Toshiro Mifune and Ursula Andress. Thanks to James Bond and *Playboy*, Ursula was someone I *did* know something about.

Both our families were staying at Hotel Aguadulce. Charlie was there with his wife, Jill, and Valentine and Jason, two of the three boys from her former marriage to David McCallum (a.k.a. Illya Kuryakin, *The Man from U.N.C.L.E.*). Jill was pregnant at the time with their first child together. She was English with long blond hair. She was beautiful.

Most fans remember Jill for her role as Leila Kalomi in "This Side of Paradise," the *Star Trek* episode in which Spock is struck by spores that cause him to release his emotions and fall in love with Leila. When we ran into the Bronsons for the first time at the hotel, Dad later told me that Charlie had visited the set one day while Dad and Jill were working on a love scene together, and Charlie was clearly not too happy. One of the crew knew Charlie from some film they had worked on together. "Hey, Charlie," the man said. "Are you going to be on this show?" Charlie's face went sour. "Are you kidding?" he said and walked off.

I hung out with Val and Jason regularly even though they were much younger. Although we were on the Costa del Sol, Hotel Aguadulce was basically in the middle of nowhere and there was not much to do. One afternoon, after we'd spent most of the day by the pool, Jill and the boys were packing up to go back to their suite when Jill asked if I'd like to come with them. Gulp. I asked my mom if it was okay.

They had a really beautiful suite of rooms. I noticed a guitar in the corner. Jill told me it was Val's and that Jason used to have one until he put his foot through it during a tantrum. She said this as she looked at Jason with what can only be described as loving disapproval. I told her I had a guitar of my own back in L.A., and she asked me if I wanted to play something. Gulp, gulp. It was afternoon and I remember the Spanish light glowing through the balcony windows. I also distinctly remember trying to stay calm as I reached for that guitar. Jill said she was taking lessons herself but that she didn't like bar chords because they were too hard for her to play. I tried to think of a song that didn't have too many bar chords. And then I sat on her bed and played a pretty damn good version of Neil Young's "Tell Me Why." I was nervous as hell, but as I played, I was relieved to hear that song come out of me with absolute perfection. And there was only one bar chord. I played that song for Jill. Jill Ireland. I sat on her bed and played her my song. Neil's song.

And she loved it.

———

The following week, Jill invited our family to join hers for dinner in the hotel dining hall. During the meal, Dad asked

Charlie and Jill if they would lend us the tutor they had brought along for their children so that he could work with my sister, Julie, and me. We were in Spain during the school year and Julie and I had homework and we weren't doing it. All eyes turned to Charlie for his reply and he did not look happy. In fact, he scared the shit out of me.

"We paid for him to fly out with us and we pay him a salary and expenses." Charlie was terse, but the street kid from Boston wasn't giving in.

"I realize that," Dad replied. "That's why I'm willing to reimburse you for part of it."

Charlie sat motionless like they were in some poker game and Dad had just upped the ante. The Italians didn't call him "Il Bruto" for nothing, because Charles Bronson was one mean-looking motherfucker, with beady eyes and stony features. In fact, I always thought he was a tougher-looking version of Dad. The dining hall was dark, which really set the mood for the showdown.

The room was crowded and noisy but no one said anything at our table as Charlie pondered Dad's offer, looking like his hand-grenade persona might explode at any minute. And then Jill stepped in:

"Please, Charlie, Steve has plenty of free time and the boys don't need him all day."

That's when I fell apart. That's when I turned to mush. That's when I completely fell for Jill Ireland, this gorgeous Englishwoman who was once married to Illya Kuryakin.

Charlie just sat there in some sort of funk like Jill had just told him no sex until he agreed.

"Let me think about it."

Those were his last words on the subject as I dug into my

flan and stole a look at Jill. She had this self-satisfied smile like she was going to keep at him until he gave in.

In the end, Julie and I worked every weekday with Steve, the Bronsons' funny tutor from UCLA who could play "Light My Fire" on his mouth accordion.

Jill died in 1990 after a long battle with breast cancer. She was fifty-four.

JUST TELL ME IT'S NOT OVER

JONAH REGULARLY MAKES me take him to the pound after school to check out who's there: to see who's new, who's been there a while, and who's missing, either because they've been adopted or "alleviated."

We pass by one of the cages and there's a new kid on the block, a dachshund-Chihuahua mix: small, short-haired, brown, shorter body than a dachshund but higher off the ground, big floppy ears, tail wagging, little snout. He's smiling at us. The ears don't quite stand up like a Chihuahua's, but flap around like he might fly off at any moment. The eyes smile along with the mouth and the tail never stops. Mr. Personality. We can tell right away he's a winner and will likely survive the pound experience.

The adoption date says he's available on Monday. I have resisted every dog up to this point, but Jonah is so desperate, he's even been online looking at pugs and Boston terriers because that's what he thinks he wants. I keep putting him off because he's got enough animals, with Zero the black cat, Serafina the calico, and Buddy the golden retriever, who will bark at his own shadow for hours. But Jonah wants to complete the set, because he says three doesn't make sense: If it was okay to have two cats, why not two dogs? And I know he's doing it in part to help fill the void I left behind and I can't really blame him. So I figure what the hell, I don't live there anymore anyway, he can have as many animals as he wants. And that little dog sitting on death row is pretty darn cute—but Jonah will have to deal with his mother on this because even though Nancy and I have been working very hard to get along for the benefit of the kids, there is no way I'm going to try to convince her to take on a new animal.

At first, Nancy vehemently resists the idea, but Jonah grinds her down until she finally agrees to drive to the pound to take a look. And on Monday morning at 7 AM, Nancy is there. She'd be the first to admit to having trouble being anywhere at that hour. But for Jonah, and that little, smiling dog, she is there.

They named him Otto because of the dachshund in him. It was a toss-up between that and Tito, for the Mexican side, but the Germans won out.

———

I'm now on my way to The Apple Pan to meet a friend for a burger. The Pan is one of the few things left in West L.A. that's older than me.

Just as I arrive, I get a call from Maddy. She's been on edge lately because she's struggling in science and this week, she has to swim in PE at 7:30 AM and it's freezing and she doesn't have time to shower and get the chlorine off and put her lotion on.

This morning she had a little breakdown when I came to pick her up but I managed to get her to school on time. And I made a good lunch for her. She told me she loves my lunches because I put different things in them. And she seemed okay when I dropped her off, but Nancy had to pick her up early because she wasn't feeling well.

Now it's 1 PM and she's calling me on my cell, crying hysterically, and through the tears I can just about make out what she's saying: that Nancy said we were starting to see other people and why can't you come home, Dad, and it's been almost a year and it's been long enough . . . and that she needs me and Jonah needs me, especially for his Bar Mitzvah, and please don't tell me it's over, Dad, please say it's not over, please, Dad, please.

I tell her how sorry I am that she's having a hard time and that she needs to calm herself down and this is why we need to go to therapy to talk about all this. I tell her I'm at lunch and that I'll call her afterward, and she starts to calm down and says okay and we hang up.

When I pick Jonah up from school, she calls him on his cell. While he's sitting in the car, I can hear her voice. She still has a sweet little voice, just like when she was a little girl, only now Maddy's fourteen and a half. She's saying things to her little brother that I can hear through the phone.

"And guess what?"

"What?"

"We got Otto a collar with dog bones on it and we got him a name tag and a bed and guess what else?"

"What?"

"We signed him up for dog training and you're going to take him to Rancho Park on Saturday."

And when we get to the house, Maddy's so much better. But when I sit down next to her and put my arms around her, she whispers to me, "Please tell me it's not over. Please tell me."

But I can't tell her because it *is* over. Even though Nancy and I are getting along, I know with absolute certainty there's no going back. Nancy and I decided not to tell the kids until after Jonah's Bar Mitzvah, which is coming up. These days I don't even discuss divorce with Nancy.

But when the Bar Mitzvah is over, a long, troubled marriage is finally going to come to an end.

SMILE FOR THE CAMERA

IN THE WINTER of 1967, it poured. My sister Julie and I came home from school one day and we were drenched. We still lived on Comstock, and when we got home there was a photographer waiting for us. This was after *16 Magazine* published our home address as Dad's fan mail address and, as usual, there were stacks of fan letters on the dining room table as well as the prefab autographed pictures. You could get a picture of Dad with or without Spock makeup, but the Spock pictures were the most popular.

So we walked into the house dripping and Mom and Dad were there and there was this photographer waiting to take some family photos for a TV magazine, photos of the happy family answering all that fan mail. Julie and I looked at each other because we couldn't believe it, and we turned to Mom and Dad. "We can't take pictures. Look at us. We're soaked!"

Now, with me it wasn't so bad—I could dry my hair and get on with it. But Julie . . . Julie had the most beautiful long brown hair and it was a mess. Dad was his usual energetic, blustery self. "Come on, it's gonna be great!" Julie and I were laughing because it was so ridiculous. But we did it—and we smiled while we did it.

But by far my favorite family picture was the formal portrait we took not long after we moved to Westwood in the fall of 1968. It was probably around 1970, and Dad was on *Mission:*

Impossible. The photographer was setting up in the living room. Julie and I were in the kitchen griping about the fact that neither of us was in the mood. We were in our teens by then and maybe we were getting a little ornery, and we both had had enough of the picture taking.

The house in Westwood was much bigger than the house on Comstock. My parents and Julie had rooms upstairs and I was downstairs with my own bathroom and a door to the backyard that three years later, Chris Kelton and company would occasionally plow through on a Saturday night looking to party. We weren't living in such close quarters anymore and the family was drifting apart. I never really considered ours a "close" family anyway: It was more like there was Mom and Julie and then there was me and then there was Dad. He was rarely around because he was always either working or looking for work. Nor was he participating in the functioning of the family and Mom alone couldn't make it happen. Add to that the drug and alcohol abuse that would soon consume the men in the family and then the long decline of my parents' marriage and you have the quintessential dysfunctional family. And now we had to have our picture taken, and from Julie's and my perspective, it was a little like, "Hell, no, we won't go!"

"Julie and Adam!" Dad was calling us from the living room. It was one of those calls where you weren't supposed to answer, you were simply supposed to report for duty. But we stayed in the kitchen. My mother came to get us. She asked us to not make trouble. And so we went in.

"Come on, it's gonna be great!"

But it wasn't.

And so we sat for the picture. And there wasn't a smile among us. It's my favorite family portrait. Because it's the truth.

MONICA

I FELL FOR Monica the second she first walked into the Monday night meeting: beautiful face, long dark hair, tight jeans. I elbowed Justin, and when he saw her he nodded. Then she started coming regularly, and when she volunteered to take the coffee commitment, Justin and I turned to each other and said in perfect unison, "She's in." Monica has the most gorgeous body and legs that go on forever. And she's got the postmodern-hippie-chick look down to a fine art: the toe rings, the sandals, the tight ripped jeans, the faux-diamond-studded belt buckle, the tank tops, the blouses, the corduroy jacket with just a hint of fur fringe, the Hello Kitty purse. I mean, sometimes I'd go to the meetings just to see what Monica was wearing. And best of all, she's in her mid-forties! She has the lines of age—I'm a sucker for attractive women who have the lines of age. Sometimes I'd catch her looking at me and we'd smile at each other.

After several weeks, I finally break the ice and start talking to her. From then on, all of our conversations are about . . . her. But I try to listen attentively and ask pertinent questions. And because my name starts with an *A* and I happen to be at the top of the Anonymous phone list, Monica will sometimes call to say she can't be at the meeting and will I take her coffee commitment and she leaves these voice-mail messages that go on and on until she's cut off. Then she calls back and continues on until she's cut off again. And she smokes like a fiend—her car is like a moving ashtray. But I still like to look at her.

One night I caught her staring at me probably because I was wearing a vintage, dark green paisley shirt that I've had for years. After the meeting, some guy went up to her to get a cheap thrill from a free hug, but she kept her eye on me. She quickly finished him off and came over. We held each other tight and I kissed her cheek and she told me how good I looked.

That's when I forgot who she was and began to think she could be mine.

Sometimes I think I want her so badly that when I pass her apartment, I yell out her name, just in the privacy of my car, I scream out her name, "Monicaaaaaa!"

And then I see myself standing in the rain, on the street, below her third-story balcony, calling for her, aching for her. "Monicaaaaa!"

And she comes out and calls my name and we'd be locked in this torrential love hurricane.

"Dude. Dude! She's insane." This is Justin's mantra on Monica because he's talked to her several times as well.

But I stick it right back at him. "Dude, your girlfriend's insane. She stalks you and hacks into your e-mail and calls me to find out where you are."

"Yeah, but I'd rather have Helena's insanity then an AA chick's insanity."

"Oh, man, that's just fucking insane."

———

I decide to call Monica and ask her to go clothes shopping with me to help me find some things. Clothes shopping with her seems innocent enough, like she's just a friend helping me out. And she's really into the idea and says she'll meet me at the

Santa Monica Promenade. She warns me she looks like a slob and to be prepared.

And I get to the Promenade and she's already there and I spy her from a distance and she is gorgeous: the tan Uggs, the tan legs that go on forever, the short blue-jean skirt, the tight white ribbed sleeveless T-shirt, the silver jewelry wrapped around her neck, that beautiful long brown hair.

We're in the Levi's store and she's looking at jeans and she asks me my size and then she picks out a pair for me, like she's my girl and she's been doing this forever. I try them on and I tell her they're too tight.

"How tight? Let me see."

She lifts my shirt and pulls on the waist and has her hands in my pants, real matter-of-factly, like she's been doing this for years, like we've been a couple for years and she's had her hands down my pants about a million times. But to me, it doesn't feel like a million times, it feels like I'm getting turned on.

I stand on the platform in front of the mirror and she has me turn to her and she kneels down to check out the length, and I look in the mirror and from my point of view, her back's to the mirror and she's on her knees and it looks like she's going down on me. I look down to see all that silver jewelry lying on top of her breasts and this is really getting out of control: My blood is pumping and I'm starting to sweat and it feels like I'm hyperventilating and I have to bite my knuckle when she's not looking to feel the pain so that I can get a grip and avoid the hard-on.

After I buy the jeans, we walk to Starbucks for a cup of coffee. As we walk through the Promenade, it feels good to have her by my side. While we're waiting in line for coffee, I tell her I need a girl like her. She smiles in a way that tells me she might be willing to be that girl.

That's when I hear him again.

"Dude, don't do it. She's insane."

She orders iced coffee and I get hot tea. She wants to sit outside and we walk to a nearby bench. We talk about her new job and her ex-boyfriend. Then she turns to me and says, "Do you want to go to a movie sometime?"

The afternoon sun hits her in such a way that, for the first time, I can see her eyes are green, an opaque milky-white green. I've never seen eyes like that before. We're sitting on a park bench on the Promenade and she's asking me out on a date: tight T-shirt, silver necklaces, jean skirt, legs that go on forever—and she just asked me out.

I look down at her hands because I need to breathe. And she's sitting pressed against me on that park bench. I look down at her hands and then I look back up into those green eyes, those milky green eyes.

"Yeah, a movie sounds great."

But wait a minute. There's something on her arm. I thought I saw something on her arm. I look again.

"Oh, that's a cigarette burn. I did it to myself when my last boyfriend broke up with me. I was so depressed I wanted to hurt myself."

I take her arm and run my fingers over her scar, just to caress her arm, just to feel her insanity.

Jonah calls me. He needs a ride home. I hug Monica good-bye and we go our separate ways.

FATHERS AND SONS

ON MONDAY MORNING I pick up Jonah and take him to school. I insist that we go to see his social studies teacher after school so we can all look through his class notebook. There's going to be a notebook check next week, a big part of his grade, and notebook checks have been a problem for Jonah and it would be nice if he got it right this time, particularly because he has a solid D in Mrs. Graham's social studies class. The D is actually an improvement over his last progress report in which he received an F, although I was mystified as to how he could be failing the class while also receiving an "Excellent" grade for his work habits and an "Excellent" grade for his class participation.

It turns out Mrs. Graham made a technical mistake when inputting the grades and forgot to fix it and half the class received an F.

Jonah says it's because she's "on crack." Having taught at the school and having chaperoned a number of school field trips, I know Mrs. Graham can sometimes be "idiosyncratic," but I'm pretty sure she's not on crack. So I ask him not to repeat that comment. To anyone.

We meet with her after school and she goes through his notebook and she's very frustrated that there are so many assignments missing or incomplete. Jonah's clearly embarrassed as he tries to explain himself. I try to humor her and assure her we're going to get it together by next week, because the fact of the matter is, Mrs. Graham may not be on crack but she really is erratic and overbearing at times.

When we finally walk out of her classroom, he hugs my waist.

"Thank you so much, Dad."

"You're welcome."

"You must hate me."

"Why would I hate you?"

"You must think I'm stupid."

"I don't think you're stupid, just disorganized, and now that I've substituted here off and on all year I know that Mrs. Graham is also disorganized, and when you have two disorganized people you have trouble and that's why I'm here to help you."

We get into the car and he leans against me and puts his head on my chest.

"I really mean it, Dad. Thank you so much."

I hug his head and kiss him.

———

I'm in Carol's office. She's a licensed social worker I go to for therapy once in a while.

"If your dad wasn't around when you were younger, and there wasn't such great modeling from him anyway, where did you learn your parenting skills?"

"My mother. Her love has always been unconditional. And from my mother's parents. My grandfather was very loving and so was my grandmother, even though she was this Jewish orthodox fruitcake who always yelled at my grandfather and treated my mother very badly in part because we didn't keep kosher.

"I also happen to come from the Rift Valley in East Africa, so I have the benefit of six million years of parenting evolution working for me."

"I'm not sure I believe that part of it."

"Most people don't believe that crap. But I do."

REVELATIONS

"DAD, WHY ARE you late!"

It's 7:10 AM as Maddy climbs into my car and we take off.

"Maddy, I'm here every morning at seven sharp. This is the first time and we can still make it."

"I just can't be late to school."

"You won't be."

I push a couple of lights going down Overland Avenue and manage to get on the freeway in record time. But there's traffic heading west on the 10, as usual, and I have to really focus to maneuver through it. Sometimes it gets hairy, especially when people make lane changes right in front of you and they're going much slower than you are. Like the Toyota that just came out of nowhere without signaling so I have to slam on the brakes.

"Dad, why don't you honk at him?"

" 'Cause it's not going to make any difference and I'm trying to help create a honk-free environment."

"Dad, James told me you've been going over to his house every Thursday night."

Talk about not signaling, I sure as hell didn't see this coming. We've started a Thursday night meeting at Chris Kelton's house and I'm the secretary. We meet on the back porch. Chris, his neighbor Michael, and two or three others have been showing up regularly. I knew I was going to have to tell Maddy sometime, I just didn't think it was going to be now, while I'm dodging and weaving through traffic.

"Dad, why are you going over to Chris and James's?"

"Because we're having a meeting there, honey."

"What kind of a meeting?"

"An Alcoholics Anonymous meeting."

"You're in Alcoholics Anonymous?"

"I've been going to meetings for almost a year."

"Why are you in Alcoholics Anonymous?"

I guess this is as good a time as any. I mean, Maddy's fifteen now, and I know there's been pot around, because they all start right around this age. I know I did. We've been going to therapy so this is something we are definitely going to get into. I'm pretty good at multitasking so while one side of my brain continues to focus on flying down the freeway, the other side takes the plunge.

"Honey, I'm in AA because I used to smoke pot."

"I knew you used to smoke, Dad, but I thought that was a long time ago. When was the last time you smoked pot?"

"Last year."

Surprisingly, Maddy doesn't seem particularly fazed by this as she sits there in her sandals and cut-off jeans that are way too short.

"Did you do it a lot?"

"Too much."

"Why do you go to AA if you just smoked pot?"

"Because it's all related."

We're off the freeway now and I manage to make it through two stoplights and get her to the drop-off lane on time. She pulls her stuff together and opens the car door.

"Are you okay with what I just told you?"

"I don't know."

"Well, how do you feel about it?"

"I don't know, Dad. I have to think about it and I don't want to be late."

"Do you need any money?"

"No, Mom made me lunch. Who's picking me up?"

"I am. I'll get Jonah first and then come and get you."

"Okay, Dad. See ya later. Loves you."

"I loves you too, honey. Have a good day."

————————

In the afternoon, I go to pick up Jonah from middle school. We stop at a Starbucks drive-through and there's a bit of an incident because Kirsten is there, this pretty little blonde who's wearing a puka shell necklace. Jonah's had a crush on her since he started middle school. He wrote her a note saying he wanted to offer her his heart, but Maddy put the kibosh on that right away, explaining to him that Kirsten wouldn't want him to say something like that.

He still has a thing for her because he's hiding in my car so she won't see him.

"Should I honk my horn and wave, Jonah?"

"Dad, I swear if you do that I'm going to be so mad."

I know that a part of him wants me to do it but I let it go.

We pick up Maddy. As usual, she's starved when we get her, but today I don't have my cold pack, so I agree to take them to a rib joint. We get there and decide what to order. Maddy looks up from her menu.

"Dad, restaurants are really trusting."

"What do you mean?"

"They let you order and eat the food before you have to pay."

"That's kind of funny, honey. I guess you can look at it that way." Then I reach over and squeeze her earlobe. "Maddy, you're so cute. You got ears, Maddy. Jonah, Maddy's got ears."

When I finish squeezing, and we finish ordering, Maddy looks to Jonah.

"Dad's in Alcoholics Anonymous."

"What? You are? I don't believe it! What's Alcoholics Anonymous?"

I answer him. "It's for people who want to stop drinking alcohol usually because they drink too much and get drunk."

Maddy again. "Dad's been going to Chris and James's house for AA meetings. And you're not drinking anymore, Dad?"

"No, honey."

"Not even beer?"

"Not even beer."

"Why not?"

"Because I don't like it anymore. I don't need it."

"But I thought you said you smoked too much."

"It's all related, honey."

"And you're never going to drink again?"

"I wouldn't say never. But I'm pretty sure I'm not going to be drinking today or tomorrow."

Maddy is silent now as she processes the information. She's changed so much this past year, she's getting older. And I know she's at the right age to be talking about this stuff, Jonah too for that matter. But then again, they both seem so young to be thinking about smoking and drinking.

It's just the three of us in a booth—otherwise the place is empty because it's four in the afternoon. It's kind of nice having the place to ourselves, just me and my two kids. Our appetizer arrives: an iceberg wedge with a dollop of blue cheese dressing on the side. Maddy and I are sharing it and our taste buds go wild.

"But, I really don't get it, Dad. I mean, you never had a problem drinking, like Brian Jameson and Michael Dayton. I mean, I can tell that they drink a lot but I never saw you drink that much."

"No, but when I did drink, I usually got a little drunk, and then I always wanted to smoke afterward. That's why it's all related."

Jonah's food arrives. As usual, there is nothing that resembles a vegetable on his plate.

"Jonah, when are you going to start eating things that are organic?"

He points to the French fries. "The potato came from the ground."

———

"So what's your concern?"

It's Shayna talking now. She's the new therapist that Nancy found. I like Shayna and so do the kids because she's a tough, fair-minded New York Jew who likes to say "Fuck that" and "Who needs that shit?"

Maddy and I are in Shayna's office.

"My concern is that I'm a pothead and I don't want my daughter to become one."

"I don't do it that much, Dad."

Shayna takes charge.

"Well, Maddy, let me tell you. I have worked with kids for years in Twelve-Step programs like the one your dad is in. And because of the research on this, I can tell you that your dad has a valid concern, because kids who have parents who are alcoholics or addicts have between a forty and seventy percent chance of becoming one themselves, depending on whether one or both parents have a problem. Maddy, do you see using pot as a problem?"

"No, I hardly do it, like, just on the weekends with my friends, and I don't take that much."

Me now. "But you told me some time ago when I asked you about it that Anna smokes every day."

"Yeah, but that's because she's got this messed-up life because her parents are, like, divorced and her dad has a new wife and doesn't pay very much attention to her. But I'm not doing it every day, just with my friends."

"And what about Renata and Janey. I know they get high regularly."

"Yeah, but I'm not that close to either of them and they have problems in school and that's just not me, Dad."

Shayna turns to me. "As you probably already know from your own experience, there's weed all over this town. And there's simply no way for kids to avoid it, because just about everybody knows somebody or a friend of a friend or whatever who does it. And a policy of zero tolerance doesn't solve the problem because then the kid oftentimes smokes out of defiance. It doesn't sound like it's a problem or out of control for Maddy. What's good is that you guys are talking about it openly and that, Maddy, you know your dad had a problem that he's now working hard to take care of, and it actually wouldn't be a bad idea for you to maybe go with your dad to one of the meetings he goes to just to see what it's like."

"Well, yeah, it turns out I have to go to an AA meeting, because at Teen Line [where Maddy volunteers to answer phones to give free counseling], they require us to go to an AA meeting."

And that's how the sobriety thing was broached with Maddy, who seemed much more interested in it than Jonah. Then again, when I was listening to him and his friends jamming out back in the studio where I used to get high all the time, Jonah stopped drumming and announced, "Yeah, my dad used to smoke [he pretends to puff on a spliff] weed but he's in AA and doesn't do it anymore."

So nice when a kid is proud of his old man.

ICONS HAVE FEELINGS TOO

I'VE NEVER HAD much luck arguing with him. Have you ever argued with a Pop Culture Icon? Have you ever argued with a guy who can cause a frenzy among thousands at a convention hall simply by giving the Vulcan hand salute?

Because when you're dealing with a man who's adored by millions of fans the world over, fans with no need to differentiate between Spock and Leonard, when you lock horns with a man from the tenement streets of Boston who clawed his way to the top of the Hollywood heap, good luck with the argument.

Star Trek IV was a pretty good movie. One of the best in the franchise. Dad starred in it and directed it. Pretty remarkable when you think about it. I knew there was stuff going on during the preproduction period that was really bothering him, clashes with the producers over the usual creative issues. It was also around this time that my parents' marriage began to fall apart, and it wasn't long before Dad moved out of the house. And on one particular Friday night, Dad needed to blow off some steam.

I went to pick up my parents from the house in Westwood. We were going to the movies. He was mad at me because I was rushing him. I still do that sometimes. I'll rush people to get somewhere, and then when we get there, we find there was no reason to rush. As Mom and I waited in the car, Dad was puttering around. He seemed to be making a point by keeping us waiting. When he finally got in the car, he really let it fly.

"I've had to put up with crap all day and I'm not going to take it from you!"

"Just because you had a bad day at the office doesn't mean you can take it out on me!"

We ended up in a parking lot in Westwood where the argument continued. I finally walked away from him as he stood there yelling at me. I went to the movie. Dad and Mom took a cab home.

The theater was half empty and the movie started late. And it sucked.

The next night, I went over to the house to try to patch things up. He was standing in the living room in his signature brown cotton bathrobe and slippers. There was a highball glass with just the ice left sitting on the coffee table. He was just as angry and accusatory as the night before. After the first volley, just for extra emphasis, he stepped right up to my face.

"Step back, Dad."

"Why should I?"

"Because I'm not comfortable with you this close to me. Step away from me."

We were standing in a dark corner of the living room. I could smell the Johnny Walker on his breath. Up to that point, I had always believed there was no comparison between pot and alcohol: You can maintain while under the influence of pot more so than you can with booze. But while we were standing there, I began to see that Dad was just like me: just trying to feel warm and fuzzy inside, just trying to fill that big black hole in his life with a glass of Johnny.

"Get away from me, Dad."

He finally backed off, walked over to the couch and sat down in a daze. I also sat down on the couch but at a distance. I apologized for rushing him the night before but tried to explain that this had just as much to do with the other things going on in his life.

"Just give me an inch, Dad. That's all I'm asking for. Just take an inch of responsibility for what's happening here. I'm begging you."

But he refused.

It would be nearly another twenty years before I would learn in recovery that when you offer an apology, you don't look for one in return.

Unable to get through to him, I went upstairs to say good night to my mother. On my way out, from the entry hall, I called to him: "I hope we can talk some more later."

Through the living room doors, I spied an often distant and lonely man standing in his bathrobe with his back to me. A man who had great difficulty expressing his feelings other than through anger and resentment.

He barely turned to me with his reply.

"Yeah, okay."

———

And this is what invariably happens when I'm going through one of these cycles of conflict with him:

The next day I'm at the cleaner's. "Hi. I forgot my receipt but I'm picking up some shirts."

"What's the last name?"

"Spelled N-i-m-o-y."

"Nimoy? Any relation?"

"Yeah."

"Oh, yeah, I can see the resemblance. Is he your father?"

"Yeah."

"Oh, my God. I'm a huge *Star Wars* [sic] fan. What was it like growing up the son of Dr. Spock [sic]?"

"Oh, it has its ups and downs. Just like everything else in life, I guess."

"Oh, my God. I gotta tell my [wife, husband, brother, sister, father, mother, cousin, friend]. I am a really huge, huge fan. And I've got to tell you, your father saved my life when I was in college. I don't know how I would've gotten through without him."

"Yeah, that's great. Listen, I'm kind of in a hurry. Do you think I can get my shirts?"

GOD CAN CHANGE YOU

MORE TROUBLE IN school for Jonah: He just received a progress report and he got some seriously bad grades. I pick him
up from school. He says not to worry, it's just the beginning
of the semester and he can fix the problem. I let him have it.
I tell him how I'm sick of his excuses when it comes to his
homework: It's always "I forgot" or "She never told us" or "It
wasn't on the board" or "I left it at Michael's" or "I handed it in
but she lost it" or "It was right here a second ago, I think Buddy
[the dog] took it." I remind him of all the times I've offered to
take him to the library but he never wants to go. I tell him how
sometimes I'll be looking for him and he'll be off skateboard-
ing somewhere while all his friends are at home studying. I tell
him I'm sick and tired of hearing his excuses.

All of this hits him hard and he gets really upset and starts
to cry. He looks at me with anger through the tears.

"You have no idea how much I hate you right now!"

And as I turn away from him I'm thinking, *You have no
idea how much I hate myself right now.*

It's just so damn painful to see my long-haired boy sitting in
my car on such a beautiful spring day crying and hating me. I
start thinking about my dad and how he was always working
and barely paid attention when he wasn't.

Now I have to drag him to the rabbi's office because we
have to talk about his Torah portion, the section of the Old

Testament he'll be reading for his Bar Mitzvah. He has to write a speech about it too, about what it all means. He refuses to go. I apologize over and over again for coming down so hard on him, but he won't forgive me. I get him something to eat and he starts to feel better and agrees to come with me to the rabbi's office.

Rabbi Fox also officiated at Maddy's Bat Mitzvah, and the meeting in her office turns out to be really interesting. Jonah's Torah portion is about Aaron and Miriam, Moses's brother and sister, and how, while wandering in the desert, they became jealous of Moses's power and started to bad-mouth Moses and his new wife. God calls them out and gets very angry with them for gossiping about Moses. Rabbi Fox asks Jonah if there's anything going on in his life that's similar to what's happening in this story. And Jonah comes up with a couple of situations where he was accused of spreading gossip and it made some kids at school very angry with him. He says he tries really hard not to bad-mouth people, especially his friends, even if he's mad at them, because he knows it just brings trouble. Rabbi Fox seems very pleased because she's trying to show him that although the Torah is thousands of years old, it can still teach us new things about our lives today. She says that reading and studying Torah is like marinating a chicken, because it changes us and brings flavor to our lives. But what we don't realize while we're sitting in her office is that Jonah *is* that chicken. Because when the meeting is over, and Jonah and I are driving out of the parking lot, he starts singing,

"God can change me, but da, da, da, da." He's singing to the tune of David Bowie's "Changes" and I say, "What was that?!" And he sings it again, "God can change me . . ." And then he says, "Dad, I don't know all the words but isn't that a David Bowie song?" And I say, "Yeah, it's a Bowie song. It's Bowie's

'Changes,' but the lyrics are *'Time may change me,'* not *'God can change me.'* " And then I turn to him and say, "Dude"—because all middle school boys call each other "Dude"—"you just had a spiritual experience." He just sits there and smiles.

I drive him back to the house and I try to get him to crank out a first draft of his speech based on his discussion with the rabbi. I'm praying that God really *has* changed Jonah and that he won't give me a hard time. But he insists that he's entitled to some downtime, and he picks up his guitar and starts jamming to AC/DC. And now I'm really getting pissed and it's here we go again. Nancy appears with a manila envelope addressed to the parents of Jonah Nimoy from the principal's office and I'm thinking, *Oh, boy, this is it. It's back to academic probation, and what the hell am I going to do with this kid?* I mean, it's great that he's bound for rock 'n' roll glory, but how am I going to educate this kid?

Only it's not academic probation. It's a letter from the principal congratulating Jonah on his academic excellence, with a certificate confirming his outstanding scholastic achievement. He looks at me like he just took a happy pill and says, "See, Dad, I told you."

He waltzes out of the room wailing guitar riffs to "Hell's Bells."

I turn to Nancy.

"There must be some mistake."

TYPICAL CONVERSATION WITH
A TEENAGE DAUGHTER #214:
JAMES AGAIN

"DAD, I STILL can't believe James is coming to Jonah's Bar Mitzvah."

"Maddy, you've been carrying on about this for weeks and I don't want to hear it."

"Why not?"

"Because you're just going to have to deal with it."

"But why did you invite him?"

It seems that Maddy and James have been on-again, off-again for some time but I haven't been able to figure out if they were dating or are just good friends and I don't ask Maddy because I don't want to put her on the spot. I have no idea what sparked the love-to-hate situation, but now methinks my daughter doth protest too much.

"Maddy, you know why I invited James. Because Chris is a good friend of mine and James comes with Chris. If the Bar Mitzvah were last year, you wouldn't have any problem having James there. In fact, you'd be all atwitter about it."

"Well, I'm not now. I can't stand him. And I can't believe you still have his phone number in your cell phone."

"That's because you used to be with him 24/7."

"That is so untrue."

"Maddy, don't start. I couldn't tear you away from that guy.

When you first met him at the skating rink, you were so excited. And then you hung out with him all last summer. You guys were inseparable and all your girlfriends were in love with him. When I started going to meetings at Chris's house, you had me pick you up and take you with me just so you could spend an hour watching *The O.C.* with him."

"Dad, that is such a lie."

"Oh, Maddy. The fact is, even though I think that you still really like him . . ."

"That is *so* false. I hate him, Dad. You *know* I hate him! He is so mean now and I don't care if I never see him again."

"Whatever. The point is you're very lucky you got to know him and worked through some of your feelings for him and decided he might not be the guy for you. There were so many girls in high school that I was interested in and I know they were interested in me but I never found out what they were like and whether or not I really wanted to be with them."

"Why didn't you find out?"

"Because I was too nervous and shy and I didn't know what the hell I was doing. Debbie Whelan, Laurie Cherney, Kyle Phillips. I should have hung out with all of them, and just thinking about them now still drives me a little crazy. Consider yourself lucky that you had your little fling with James and you got over him, sort of, and just leave the poor guy alone. He's had enough trouble in his life with both his parents being addicts."

"I just wish he wasn't coming to the Bar Mitzvah."

"He's coming along with 225 of our closest friends, so you'll have plenty of people to talk to so you can ignore him."

Maddy finally goes silent. I think I'm getting through to her. This seems to be sinking in.

"But, Dad, why did you invite him?"

ALL'S FAIR IN LOVE
AND WORLD WAR II

IT WAS THE winter of '73. Or maybe it was '74. There's a Web site that can tell me the exact date but I can't find it right now. Dad was on Broadway, starring in an Otto Preminger production of Erich Maria Remarque's *Full Circle.* It's an obscure play about an escaped political prisoner running from the horrors of World War II and ending up with a woman he has to convince to hide him. Bibi Andersson played the woman. She was from Sweden and I knew she was in a lot of Ingmar Bergman movies. Bibi was hot in that classy, silk blouse, European kind of way. The play was good, and Dad was very good, all grubby from the war, his clothes torn, a Lugar pistol in his hand. He was desperate to get away after spending seven years in the prison camps, and he had to convince Bibi to hide him. Would she? Would she fall in love with him and keep him safe? Or would she betray him to save herself?

I used to have a photograph of Dad and Bibi smiling as they aimed their Lugars at Otto Preminger's big, fat, bald head. He was the director of the play and he sat with a glass of booze in his hand looking totally bombed. They were onstage, the three of them. Dad and Bibi were smiling with such glee as they pointed their pistols at Otto because they pretty much hated Preminger. Dad said his directing style consisted of barking orders at the actors. He'd yell in his German accent, "Ze lines! You must learn ze lines!"

Dad told me that one night after rehearsal, he went to a bar for a quick drink when two hot numbers sidled up to him.

"Your place or ours?" one of them asked.

"Thanks," Dad said, "but I have to go home and learn my lines."

The next day, when he told this to Preminger, the director blurted, "For all ze lines you learned, you shuud have fuct!"

I really loved that play. They were so good together, Dad and Bibi. Despite the tough subject matter, you could just tell that they really enjoyed playing the parts. I hoped that one day I could play at my work the way that they did at theirs.

Afterward, Dad took me around to meet her. We were standing at her dressing room door when he introduced me. At close range she was overwhelming. Petite and pretty in her camel hair skirt and creamy white blouse, with her sweet smile and her Swedish accent. And then suddenly, Liv came to mind. Bibi immediately reminded me of Swedish actress Liv Ullmann. I had recently seen a movie trailer of Liv in *The Emigrants,* and now I couldn't get Liv out of my mind but I made a conscious decision not to mention her name.

I remember a lot about that night. Some things from the past I can remember very well. Sometimes it's a blessing, other times it's a curse. This memory is a blessing, definitely a blessing, as we stood outside her dressing room. She was so attentive and glad to meet me and she never stopped giving me her sweet Swedish smile. I remember her gorgeous eyes and her charisma and the door to her dressing room and how a single overhead lightbulb lit up that musty backstage hallway at the Anta Theatre. I like to hold on to that memory of Bibi because to this day, I still feel the glow of her smile.

It was decided that we would share a taxi uptown. Bibi had to collect her things while Dad and I went outside to get the cab.

When we walked out into the night, I remember it being cold and wet. I think it was November. November in New York felt so good and different from what I was used to in Southern California. I told Dad that Bibi was beautiful and that I couldn't stop thinking about how much she reminded me of Liv Ullmann.

"It's a good thing you didn't mention Liv Ullmann. I think there's some serious rivalry between the two of them. They've both worked extensively with Bergman."

The next thing I knew, the three of us were in the backseat of a cab driving through midtown Manhattan. Bibi was squeezed in between us and I felt safe and warm sitting next to her in the shadows of that cab. She didn't waste any time as she turned her attention to me.

"Do you like older women?"

I think I was seventeen. Bibi Andersson was pressed against me as she seduced me with her Swedish accent. She was confident and natural as if this was typical European small talk. I was dumbstruck—I had no idea what to say.

But Dad knew. *He* knew what was going on. *He* knew what to say.

"Adam's had some experience with older women." He was as cool about it as she was.

She turned to me with surprise.

"Is this *troo*?"

I finally found some words.

"Yes . . . I do enjoy the company of . . . beautiful, older, Swedish women . . . especially . . . if they've worked extensively . . . with Bergman."

BAR MITZVAH TIME!

IT'S THE MORNING of Jonah's Bar Mitzvah and I arrive at the house early and whip up some eggs and toast and make everyone eat so that our blood-sugar levels will last through the service. Then we race out the door to get to the temple in time for pictures. For some reason, Jonah goes to grab the plastic ziplock bag full of yarmulkes, or skullcaps, that I always kept in a cabinet in the dining room. I bet there are a lot of Jewish homes with a bag full of yarmulkes. You end up collecting these things through the years because you forget to take them off at the temple and you don't want to throw them away, so you keep them in a plastic ziplock bag and use them for Shabbat or Passover. But there are yarmulkes at the temple so it seemed a little odd that Jonah thought to grab the ziplock bag, a bag he has never otherwise paid any attention to. As I'm driving, he's sitting in the back going through the bag, and he pulls out a purple-colored yarmulke that he says he wants to wear. He looks at the underside and it reads, "Alan Nimoy's Bar Mitzvah, July 28, 1969." It jolts me to hear him reading Alan's name. Alan was my first cousin, my father's brother's second son, who was a month older than me. Alan had cystic fibrosis, a digestive and lung disorder, and he died just after his seventeenth birthday in 1973.

"Dad, were you close to Alan?" Maddy asks.

"Alan was to me what Spencer is to Jonah." Spencer is my sister's second son, and he's very close with Jonah. And my kids seem to understand that more than thirty years ago, I lost somebody who was like a brother to me. Alan was a skinny Jewish boy, just like me; he was a good student, just like me; and he intended to go to law school, just like me. For years, I would go out to New Jersey to visit him for the summer. We told each other everything. Sometimes, when I'd look at Alan, it felt like I was looking at a sick version of myself.

————

Nancy and I sit with Maddy on the bimah, the platform where the rabbi and cantor sit. We're really enjoying the whole ceremony, showing our friends and family that nothing between us is going to spoil the moment. And even though some members of my extended family aren't speaking to others, I really don't care.

Thanks in large part to his Hebrew tutor and my constant push on Jonah to practice, he makes his way through all the prayers very beautifully. He looks like a little cherub with all that long hair and those baby-fat cheeks. When he finishes the chanting, he wipes some imaginary sweat off his forehead with a wrist sweatband I didn't even know he had brought with him.

I make my speech to Jonah from memory: about the day I took him to Guitar Center and how lucky I was to have him in my band and how he replied he was lucky to have me in *his* band; about that day in the parking lot when Jonah sang the "God version" of Bowie's "Changes" and how that qualified him as a "marinated chicken"; about how it's fun driving Jonah to school because he's like a pop-culture sponge, he's always spouting off funny dialogue from some Jim Carrey movie—although that past week there was some strange dialogue coming out of his mouth because with the passing of the pope, Jonah and some of his friends thought it would be a good idea to commemorate the event by renting *The Exorcist.*

To Nancy's credit, she suggested that in the thank-you part of Jonah's speech, he should acknowledge my aunt Sybil and uncle Mel, Alan's parents, and mention the yarmulke. When the thank-you's came, he lifted the yarmulke above his head and said with a sweet, somber voice, "Aunt Sybil and Uncle Mel, I want to thank you for coming to my Bar Mitzvah and I want you to know that the yarmulke I'm wearing today is from Alan's Bar Mitzvah."

Up on the bimah, looking out at the congregation, I can see my uncle Mel and cousins Steve and Paul looking expressionless, like they didn't hear a word of it. Then again, these guys are Nimoys: They aren't ones to express a whole lot of emotion. But when I look over at my aunt Sybil and cousin Judy, they have tears flowing. And now Nancy's crying. Actually, she's been crying through the whole thing and has already gone through my entire packet of Kleenex. And in that moment, I start thinking, *Did we do a mitzvah, a good deed, by having Jonah mention Alan? Or did we just make a huge mistake?* And now there is so much emotion rising in my chest that if I weren't a Nimoy male, I might start crying too. I look up at the etched-glass windows behind the ark that houses the Torah scrolls. The light is shining through and it's as if I can feel the hand of God rushing through my chest.

I can feel everything now, and sometimes, it's overwhelming.

———

The nighttime reception is being held at the Hard Rock Cafe. I put together a kick-ass video of Jonah's life filled with cool music and it just rocks as it plays on all the TV screens. The food is terrific, and we have a great DJ who has the kids doing the usual group activities. Throughout the evening, Jonah and various band incarnations take the stage and play rock 'n' roll. He plays his new Gibson SG that I let him buy with some of his early Bar Mitzvah money. Justin backs Jonah up on bass. It's mostly AC/DC night, and Jonah's Angus Young imitation is flawless, including the one-handed guitar riffs. Maddy gets up and sings. In between songs, the crowd in front of the stage chants, "Jonah, Jonah, Jonah . . ."

THE THERAPY POLICE

IT'S WEEKS LATER and the afterglow from the Bar Mitzvah is starting to fade. Nancy and I decide to meet at her therapist's office to talk about what's next. Actually, Hannah started out as *our* therapist, as she was the first marriage counselor we went to see before we moved on to Carol and then Patricia. Nancy stayed on individually with Hannah, which was fine with me.

I start the session by explaining what's become obvious over the last year and a half: The marriage is over and it's time to move on. Hannah says she understands and doesn't try to convince me otherwise, which is a *huge* relief. In fact, she says she and Nancy have been preparing for this for some time. There's no doubt in my mind that it's a sad ending to a relationship that had begun with so much promise.

We met at our ten-year high school reunion. I knew her at University High but we didn't hang out together. I was bored until she walked in the room. She was cool and funny and pretty. I started introducing her around as my wife. She didn't flinch. We were married eleven months later. She used to hold me in our bed at night and whisper, "How did we find each other? How did we get so lucky?"

We tried for years to get pregnant. As soon as we decided to take a break from the fertility drugs and the inseminations, Maddy was conceived the old-fashioned way. Jonah arrived as a happy accident almost exactly two years after Maddy. After the kids were born, when they became the focus of so much attention, I wasn't hearing how lucky we were to find each other anymore. And the issues that came between us grew and grew and the couples therapy failed and failed and failed.

———

So, after eighteen and a half years of marriage, it's finally over. And here we are, back in Hannah's office so many years after we began, discussing how to end it.

We talk with Hannah about how to tell the kids and we decide on the following: We both still love you, no one's to blame, we both take responsibility, we can still do some family activities together, this is the best thing to do at this point in our lives. And that's it. There's no drama in Hannah's office, and we have a united front—except that when we get back to the house and sit down with the kids, it doesn't quite go down that way.

Somewhere between Hannah's office and the house where the kids were waiting, someone decided not to follow the script. And while Nancy's yelling and the kids are crying and the dogs are barking, I remind her that this is not what we rehearsed in *her* therapist's office.

"I don't care! I changed my mind! Call the Therapy Police!"

The halls are hell. The halls are hell. Don't just do something, sit there. Sit there. Sit there. Feelings are not facts. Facts. Facts.

And so, while the kids cry and Nancy yells and the dogs bark, I head for the door.

Jonah follows me out. We stand on the porch while he hits me and cries and says he never wants to see me again. When he finally calms down, I tell him I want to take him to the skate park because I want him to work off some steam. It doesn't take much to convince him and he goes inside to get his board and his helmet and his pads. While I wait, Maddy comes out sobbing and I promise to call her later when she and Nancy have calmed down.

Jonah's quiet during the car ride to the skate park. Then he turns to me and says that even though he's not doing what Maddy did in terms of the screaming and yelling, he's still very mad about the whole thing. I tell him I completely understand.

When we get there, I park and sit in the car as he gets out and digs into the trunk for his stuff. Then he walks up to my window.

"Look at my new tips, Dad." He's showing me the tips on his skateboard.

"You bought some new tips?"

"No, my friend Dion bought them for me. He said I was nice to him and he wanted to buy them for me."

I watch him skate as I sit in my car and call the Therapy Police. I leave a message for Hannah about what happened and she calls me back within minutes. She's very supportive and reiterates much of what she said in the meeting: that Nancy checked out of the marriage years ago and has recently been working on completely letting go so that she can move on with her life. I talk to Hannah while I watch Jonah and give him the thumbs-up when he does a little trick. He waves back and smiles and I'm starting to feel better.

Hannah tells me she has a call in to Nancy but that Nancy's not calling back. Not too hard to see why. The Therapy Police are after her.

MY NEW NOT-SO-BRILLIANT CAREER:
FILM SCHOOL

A FILM EDITOR friend of mine told me to call Stan, the director of a film school in Burbank, and talk to him about a job. The public school subbing has been good for me and I've learned some interesting things along the way. But sometimes there's nothing more to subbing than taking attendance and watching videos and I just don't know how many more times I can watch *Osmosis Jones*. I do know a helluva lot about directing, with more than forty-five one-hour single-camera dramas behind me. So I called Stan and he told me to come in and we'd talk. He also asked me if I'd be willing to give a three-hour lecture to a filmmaking class about what it's like to direct television.

"Do you think you have three hours of material?"

"Are you kidding? Stan, I could talk for three days."

I'm sitting talking to Stan at his desk and it's pretty clear to me that I'm going to like this guy. Stan is tall, well over six feet, which is pretty tall for an administrator. He walks me over to the filmmaking class and asks Linda, the instructor, to sit in on my lecture so that she can evaluate where I might best fit in at the school. I get the distinct feeling she's also there to evaluate me. There are about a dozen students in the class, mostly college age. And for three hours I talk to them about directing episodic television from the very first day of preproduction until the very last day of editing.

Throughout the lecture, I interject little asides about my own experience. I tell the class that when you've finished directing and editing an episode, you'll want to have done such a good job that the producers want you back to direct another episode. And sometimes, you've had a miserable experience on a particular show but you don't let anyone know this. And on your last day there, when you're, like, in Vancouver, because you've been shooting the show up there and you're about to be taken back to the airport and your bags are in the van and you're in the production office saying good-bye to everyone, one of the producers might come up to you and say, "It was great working with you. I've got a call in to your agent to book you for another episode." And while he's saying this to you, you just smile and nod your head and tell your mouth to say the following: "Thanks, that would be great. I'm glad you're happy with the episode. I had a lot of fun and really look forward to coming back."

But, in fact, this is what's going through your mind:

"Working on this show has been one of the biggest fucking nightmares of my entire life and you're one of the biggest fucking assholes I have ever met and I can't wait to get on that fucking plane so that I never have to see your fucking face ever again!"

(Although, as it turned out, sometimes what Adam was thinking actually came out of Adam's mouth, helping to precipitate the end to an incredibly wonderful, miserable television directing career. But I don't mention this to the class.)

Anyway, Linda laughs and cries for three hours. I mean, literally, it's like I planted her to react to my material. After the class, she tells Stan I could teach almost anything: the actors, the producers, the directors. Stan sets me up to start with an acting class that meets the following evening.

I am so looking forward to teaching that class and all those talented young people and I can't wait to share my craft with them as well as some of my experiences. And I work my ass off putting together a class curriculum. I'm so excited when I'm driving out there for that first evening class. And as I walk down the hallway leading to the classroom, I think about all those beautiful, talented people who are just waiting to hang on my every word. I'm actually thinking to myself that maybe I'll be coaching the next James Dean or Natalie Wood.

And when I step into the class, there are exactly three people sitting there.

And English is their second language.

GUEST SPEAKER

JUSTIN CALLS TO ask if I want to be the guest speaker at the Tuesday night meeting at Edison Avenue. It's the first time I've been asked to speak at a meeting and my knee-jerk reaction is to say no. I've managed to share at the Monday night and Thursday night meetings, but getting up and speaking for an extended period requires a whole lot more in the revelation department. I think about it before I say anything, and I know Chris Kelton and Mitchell, my current sponsor, would want me to do it, so I say yes. Justin says I shouldn't worry, the format for speaking at these meetings is usually the same as outlined in the AA Big Book: first you talk about what it was like when you were drinking and using, then what happened to get you to stop and what it's like now. Then, in true Justin fashion, he tells me, "You'll probably get laid. And if I stay close to you after the meeting, chicks will see that we're tight and I'll probably get laid too."

The meeting is held in this community room with the usual oppressive overhead fluorescents. There are maybe forty people there. Two hot blondes arrive. They're dressed in black skirts and jackets like they've just come from their hip office jobs at the studio or the agency.

Justin walks in. He's wearing black slacks, a black jacket, and an orange silk shirt that shows his tan chest. He's also wearing black flip-flop sandals and with his long, dark hair, he looks really cool. The two blondes hit on him immediately. It's like Hugh Hefner cavorting with his bunnies.

The secretary calls the meeting to order, which snaps me out of my *Playboy After Dark* reverie. I've never been to this meeting before and I'm surprised to find that when the meeting starts, *they turn off the lights.* There's just a little desk light next to me illuminating my face as I speak, but it's weird because I'm looking out into a crowd of seated silhouettes.

I take a deep breath and tell my incredibly wonderful, miserable story.

"Hi, my name is Adam and I'm an alcoholic and an addict."

"Hi, Adam."

"I want to thank Justin for asking me to speak tonight and I want to start by saying that my recovery began on a Friday evening in December 2003. December 19, 2003, to be exact. I was in my study in the studio out back; we had converted our garage into a little studio. And there's no one around and I've had my shot of Canadian Club and my hit of Humboldt homegrown and I'm not feeling any pain and I'm typing away thinking I'm being so artistic and so creative when the phone rings.

"The voice on the other end is a neighbor of mine whom I met at the dog park. She's calling from rehab in Utah and she tells me I should stop smoking pot. She tells me it's my turn to clean up my act and start living my life instead of numbing myself every day. And then out of nowhere comes the sound of church bells. And the heavens open up and light rays start shooting down from the sky and angels sing and rainbows and butterflies appear and this huge lightbulb turns on over my head. And that was it. After years of struggling to go straight, after countless hours in therapy, after sleepwalking stoned through most of my life, all it took was that phone call.

"Putting down drugs and alcohol wasn't really that hard for me, because by then, I was ready. After thirty years of drinking and using, I was ready. But living my life once I became sober, that's been the real killer. Because a month later, I started feeling my feelings and I realized I had to do something about a marriage that even some pretty damn good counselors and therapists could not help salvage. So I left my wife and my kids and my big beautiful house and I found myself waking up in a sleeping bag on an air mattress in an empty apartment off Venice Boulevard. And for the first few months, I would wake up in the morning and think, *How the hell did I get here?*

"But I knew very well how I got there. Because, like lots of people, I started by getting high in high school. I was an introvert and I wanted to fit in and I was on the gymnastics team and most of the seniors on the team got high and when we had these pool parties at my house after the meet, they taught me how to inhale. And I had an older neighbor who knew a lot about getting high and I thought he was the coolest thing. And I had a dad who was a workaholic and was never around, so there was a lot of unsupervised freedom to do whatever I wanted. I'm from an upper-middle-class family and never had to work except that I scooped ice cream and pumped gas basically so I could buy weed or blow or ludes or shrooms or acid or whatever happened to be available. And my dad was a song-and-dance man and he'd be out of town on weekends making personal appearances at state fairs all over the country. And they'd pay him in cash and he'd 'hide' the envelope in his shoe closet. And when I discovered it, it was like finding buried treasure. It was an envelope full of cash but I only took the twenties. I'd never take the fifties or the hundreds because those are thicker and easier to notice when they're gone. And there were plenty of twenties. It was like my own personal

ATM twenty years before they were invented. Because all addicts need to find the resources to keep their habit going. The
shoe closet was mine.

"At first I drank and used because it was cool and fun. And
there were a lot of people I knew doing it too. It's amazing
how when you start drinking and using, you discover there
are so many 'cool' kids doing exactly the same thing. I came
from a family that wasn't particularly close, and I was feeling
pretty isolated at home. And for the first time in my life, I felt
like I was a part of a big family and it made me feel all warm
and fuzzy inside. And I was always able to justify getting high
because I did well in school.

"But then, as I went through my life drinking and using,
what was once fun became fun with problems, and then, decades later, while I'm still trying to re-create the fun days of my
youth, drinking and using just brought on problems.

"It wasn't that long ago when I would literally get drunk or
high and then wonder what bad thing was going to happen
to me next. I'd wake up in the morning and get the kids off
to school. But then I no longer had a job to go to because my
career crashed and burned due in no small part to my drinking
and using, and an attitude problem that came along with it. So
finally there was no job to go back to. And as my downward
slide continued, my pot and alcohol consumption escalated.

"And so I'd drop my kids off at school and go to my home
office and do the mental gymnastics: Should I take a bong hit
now or wait 'til later? Well, I can't take one now because I have
to make phone calls to look for work and I can't risk saying
something stupid on the phone if I'm stoned. I'll smoke later.
Well, I can't smoke later because if I make the calls and I have
to wait for a return call, it could come in later and that's no
good. I'll smoke in the afternoon. Well, I can't smoke in the

afternoon because that's when I have to get my kids and I don't want them to see me stoned or smell it on my breath. I'll smoke tonight. Well, I can't smoke tonight because I need to help the kids with their homework. I'll smoke after they're in bed. Well, I can't do that because then it'll be too late and I'll be up all night. Oh, fuck it! Where's my bong?!

"The other thing that's so insidious about pot smoking is that it's quite possible to never really hit 'rock' bottom, you just keep gliding along the 'soft' bottom. I mean, being stoned is not like being drunk. You have more control of your motor skills and it's easy to fool people. You just have to act straight, which makes absolutely no sense because you get stoned or high or wasted or whatever and then you go out and about your business and have to act straight? What's the freakin' point of that? So you don't really hit bottom, like some of my friends who are recovering junkies, who tell me it gets to the point where you get so desperate that you're down on your knees looking up at the sky begging God to either cure you or kill you. So I could have gone on with my miserable life taking shots of vodka or whiskey or whatever and then topping it off with a bong hit. I knew I was just checking out of my life. One time I called this big meeting to discuss my mother's financial situation with her business manager and my sister, and I totally spaced out and took a nice big bong hit that morning. I swear, while I'm holding that hit in, that's when I get the call from my sister. 'Where are you? We're all sitting here waiting for this meeting to start.'

"And my kids kept growing and suddenly, I'm having all these paranoid thoughts about their safety, that I'll do something while I'm high that'll cause them to get hurt. And then I start having these thoughts about my thirteen-year-old son who likes to surf and skateboard and play rock 'n' roll and watch back-to-back episodes of *Family Guy*. I'm thinking that someday he may discover how much more fun all those things are after you've burned down a fatty. And in my mind's eye, I could see myself coming home and smelling that sweet smell and going into my boy's room and he's there with his friends and I go up to him and ask, 'Who brought the bud?'

"And he just stands there, stoned. He stands there with his friends looking on and I can smell it on his breath and the four-foot bong is in the corner and the light streams through the bedroom giving a nice backlight to the wafting smoke. And he just looks at me with this puzzled look, and says quite simply, 'No one brought the bud, Dad. We pinched it from your stash. But don't worry, we're going to score over the weekend so we'll put it back. With interest.'

"And that's when I know I'm totally screwed, that I'm just a complete hypocrite and have no credibility whatsoever to dissuade my kid from smoking pot.

"That's why when I got that phone call on December 19, I was ready.

"And in terms of my life today, the best I can say is that I really appreciate the program. Because therapy is good for self-reflection and seeing patterns in your life and understanding why you and other people do the things you and they do. But when it comes to behavior modification, to actually making changes in your life, it's the program that's been most helpful to me. It just feels like I've done more to change my life being in recovery for the last year and a half than I have in decades of therapy. And the thing is, with drink in hand I warped my mind. With drink or pill or joint or pipe or straw in hand, I warped my mind. And have you ever seen a warped record? There ain't no way to put it back. That's why I need the steps and the readings and the sponsorship and the commitments and the meetings and the shares to help change my standard mode of thinking. I need all these things to help me deviate from neural pathways that were set in stone when I started regularly drinking and using way back when I was seventeen. That's what's so weird about becoming an addict or an alcoholic, because it's like a part of me was in arrested development and I stopped growing at the point I started drinking and using to fill this black hole in my life. And since I've stopped, it's like I'm growing feelings that I've never had before, that I'm starting to see things and experience things for the first time. And sometimes it's painful as hell. And sometimes it's just plain beautiful.

"And I can see my time is up, so thank you for letting me share."

ROLL OVER, DEAD SENATOR

I THINK I SMOKED pot just about every day during my senior year in high school. Never actually *in* school, I was way too paranoid for that, but after school, at home, I'd get wasted. I started smoking because I wanted to be social, as I was pretty much a loner up to that point. Then I fell in with a fast crowd that liked to get high, trip out at concerts, and crash parties. Unlike me, most of those people weren't terribly interested in prepping for college. But it was fun, I felt like I belonged, I had friends, I met girls.

During that period, Dad was around more and he clearly didn't appreciate my new lifestyle. I think the worst of it occurred when he tried to get one of my new friends busted for ripping off a triple-beam balance scale from his science class which we kept in my bedroom. Pretty dumb on my part, actually, because it wasn't like I was dealing, so there really wasn't any need for the scale.

When it came time to apply to college for the fall '74 term, I expressed some interest in CU Boulder, and Dad took me out there to have a look. When we took the campus tour, the words *party school* came to mind, which I thought was a little ironic. Though I was accepted at Boulder and desperately wanted to leave home, I decided I wasn't really ready to go as far as Colorado. So I settled on UC Santa Barbara, a party school much closer to home.

In the four and a half years I was in college, first at UCSB and then at Berkeley, Dad came to visit only once, which I was okay with at the time. Despite a few academic mishaps, I was doing well in school. I was smoking pot daily, ingesting whatever else I could get my hands on, and learning how to drink vast quantities of beer. I was chasing the Grateful Dead up and down the state of California. I was happy.

In 1976, responding to my good work in political science, Dad took me on a whirlwind trip to Washington, D.C. Because of his political connections, we had tea with South Dakota Senator George McGovern, lunch with Colorado Senator Gary Hart, and a meeting with newly appointed House Speaker Tip O'Neill, who offered me an internship for the following summer. We saw the sights, then drove out to Washington's home at Mount Vernon and toured Jefferson's home in Charlottesville. We were quite a sight, Dad and I: he looking sharp with his ascot, I with my hair. It was a fun trip and it felt like we were making some progress, but I was still using and he knew it. No real discussion other than his concern about me smoking paraquat, an herbicide being used in Mexico to eradicate the pot fields. When the trip was over, it was pretty much back to our separate corners.

I returned to Washington in the summer of '77 to work as an intern, which was a good way to avoid going home. I cut my hair so that I looked straighter, but I was still stoned. The internship lasted eight weeks in 100-degree heat and 100 percent humidity. I learned legislative research skills, witnessed laws being passed, and enjoyed the sights, including the college coeds who were also working in Washington that summer.

Katherine was a blind date. I think she was an undergraduate from some school in Georgia and I thought she said her dad ran a horse farm in Kentucky, but I was so stoned I honestly don't remember. I do remember she was interning for Lawton Chiles, a Democratic senator from Florida.

Katherine was petite and cute in a perky, Southern sort of way, and she had this gorgeous mane of dark hair. She was also fairly conservative. As we walked through Georgetown, she kept doing the end run so she could walk on the inside—I didn't know that men were supposed to walk on the street side of the sidewalk. She explained that this was because in yesteryear, people threw garbage out second-story windows and men were better candidates to get trashed.

But sometimes, I just can't control myself. "We have trash cans now and special trucks that come around to empty them."

When the conversation somehow turned to premarital sex, Katherine was saying stuff like, "Well, I don't know how y'all do things out in California, but where I come from, a woman is taught to save herself. I mean, I could kiss a man all night, but the rest is for my wedding night."

"Yeah, but what happens when you get to your wedding night, and you get down and dirty, and then discover that you're sexually incompatible?"

"Oh, my Lord, Adam, where did you learn your manners?"

———

I had nothing better to do the following Saturday night and I guess neither did she so we went to dinner. While I was in D.C., Dad was in New York starring in *Equus* on Broadway. I must have been drunk *and* stoned on that second date because I invited Katherine to accompany me to New York the following weekend to visit my parents. Once I realized what I had done, I figured there was no way in hell she would do it because she was so proper and I was so "wild." But Katherine said she had never been to New York. The next day, she said that, because my parents were going to be there, her daddy said she could go. On Friday afternoon, we were at National Airport boarding the shuttle.

She met my parents and we went to dinner. Katherine was sickeningly charming. Then we went to the play. I had no clue what we were in for because here was *Equus*, where the psychiatrist, played by Dad, tries to help a twisted teenage boy who, when he was about to get laid in some horse stable, freaks out and blinds all the horses with a hoof pick. And then there was the nude scene. At the end of the play, the boy starts to remember in flashback how he and the girl took off their clothes before tragedy struck. And because we're sitting in the sixth row center, the actors are literally fifteen feet away from us—buck naked. I looked sideways at Katherine, half expecting her to be averting her eyes. She was riveted.

The play was absolutely fabulous, one of the most incredible shows I had ever seen because it dealt with religion and history and psychology and passion and sex—a lot of things that I was wrestling with at the time. And it was beautifully staged, with muscular men in black stomping around in elevated platform hooves and wearing metal, shaped horse heads. Dad was brilliant as the psychiatrist: The strength of his conviction was so powerful, he was totally unrecognizable to me as my own father.

Afterward, Katherine told my parents that she found the play "stimulating."

That night, we made out in the living room of my parents' rented apartment at the Hotel des Artistes. When it was over, she went off to the guest bedroom and I slept on the couch. Her wedding night was safe.

The next morning at breakfast, she charmed my mother. When she excused herself from the table to powder her nose, Mom turned to me. "She's *so* cute!"

After breakfast, Katherine and I walked through Central Park. She became very excited at the sight of a street vendor. She wore a pea-green skirt with a poodle embroidered on it. It would have looked really cute . . . on a bobby-soxer in the '40s. When we returned to D.C., our cab dropped her off at her dorm and that was it. Did I open her door and help her with her bag? I hope so.

A few days later, I received a letter from her thanking me for such a memorable weekend. Her handwriting was perfect and so were her manners.

To this day, I try to walk on the street side of the sidewalk. And I try to be courteous and send thank-you notes. And I try not to judge people.

Unless they happen to be rednecks, jingoists, or neocons.

———

Fast-forward to the year 2000: It's December and I'm in a production office at Warner Bros. working on a script I'm about to direct. Someone in the bullpen announces there's going to be a news conference about the recent election. We all pile into the executive producer's office and watch his big-screen TV. The secretary of the state of Florida is about to make an announcement. She's about to certify the election results in favor of George Bush. She comes out of a back office and steps up to the podium. She has dark wavy hair. No effing way. No. Effing. Way. Under all that pancake, it's her.

———

Telephone call to my mother. This is going to be fun because my mother is a rabid, dyed-in-the-wool, flaming liberal.

"Hello?"

"Hi, Mom, it's me."

"Hello, son."

"Mom, do you know who Katherine Harris is?"

"Do I know who Katherine Harris is? Yes, I know who she is; she's that bitch who just handed Bush the election."

"But do you *remember* Katherine Harris?"

"What are you talking about?"

"Do you happen to remember the little Southern girl I brought to New York when Dad was in *Equus*, that little petite brunette you thought was *so* cute?"

"Ohhhhhh, noooooooooo!"

"Oh, yes."

"Well, you sure as hell didn't teach her a damn thing about politics!"

FLOWER POWER PRIESTESS

IN THE MID '60s, my mother glommed on to the aesthetics, if not the lifestyle, of "The Flower Child." There were flowers all the time in our house on Comstock. Mostly dead, dried flowers of all colors and yellow paper flowers and flower stickers on the refrigerator. My mom wore cool clothes and a "fall," which was a long-haired wig, and she wore glasses with cool frames. She was transitioning out of playing a '50s housewife into her new role as '60s Flower Power Priestess and Wife of Spock. And she was doing a pretty good job of it. She even bought a Cream album. My mom, Sandi Nimoy, went out and bought *Disraeli Gears,* which was always lying around, though I didn't listen to it very often, and when I did, I didn't really understand it. I much preferred the Fab Four, whose hit singles were far easier for a ten-year-old to comprehend.

In the fall of 1968, when *Star Trek* was in its third season, we moved into our big beautiful house in Westwood. I was twelve. We were living the good life. Shortly after the move, my mom announced we would all be going to The Forum to see Cream's Farewell Tour. Our seats were quite good—we were on the floor very close to the stage. The ushers at The Forum wore red and gold Romanesque dresses over their street clothes, which I guess were supposed to resemble togas or something. They were totally lame. The warm-up band was Deep Purple. They were good. Then Cream came on. I still wasn't really familiar with their music, but they knocked my socks off. Jack Bruce belted it out and Ginger Baker banged away like a madman at all those drumheads and cymbals. But what really amazed me was Eric Clapton. His hair was long and straight then, and I was surprised at how much he reminded me of George Harrison. And when he played, *he closed his eyes.* I couldn't understand how he could play all those notes without looking. It was as if he were playing from pure emotion and seemed to be feeling his way through every song. I was new to the concert experience and had never seen that before.

Near the end of the show, as we were standing and Cream was finishing their set, the crowd got a little rowdy and people started standing on their seats and stepping over the backs of the chairs in front of them to get closer to the stage. It was a trick I would imitate six years later when George Harrison played The Forum and I ended up standing in the front row, jumping up and down, my hands swaying and clapping in all my Krishna glory, while George sang "My Sweet Lord." Anyway, some of the hippies at the Cream show fell on us and it freaked out my parents. But because the hippies just wanted to have a good time, it didn't really bother me. Not like the fans who would come up to us while we were dining out, interrupting our family time for an autograph or to have their picture taken with Dad. For those people, I grew to have very little patience.

FROM HELL TO ETERNITY

MADDY FINALLY SLEPT over at my apartment one night with her friend Zoe. It was nice to have them here but it would be the first and last time. Jonah comes to stay with me on weekends with three or four of his friends, basically because I'm the only parent stupid enough to get up at five-thirty in the morning to take them surfing. But during the week, he stays at the house. And although I still find myself longing for them, I'm starting to get used to the separation and it's making me nervous. So I overcompensate.

On weekdays, I pick Maddy up from the house at exactly 7 AM to get her to school by 7:20. On Monday afternoon, I make sure she gets to her science tutor. On Tuesdays and Thursdays, I take her to her math tutor. On Friday, I take her cello bow in to be restrung, and on Saturday, she's having a broomball party at the local skating rink and I'm the chaperone. The party starts at 12:15 AM and ends at 1:30. At 2 AM, I'm still driving kids home. The following Friday, at 5:40 AM, I pick Jonah up to get him to Surf Club on time. Of course his gear isn't ready and I have to yell at him, but we pull it together and by 6:30 he's in the water with his surf buddies. At 7:15 AM, I wave him out, rinse him off under the beach showers, get him dressed in the parking lot, and run him up to Santa Monica High. Even though he's still in middle school, he's the featured solo guitarist on "Stairway to Heaven" backed by the Santa Monica High School orchestra, including Maddy on cello. He's got to be at rehearsal by 7:30. At 8:15 I run him over to Donut King for breakfast, then over to John Adams Middle School. I drop his surfboard and his guitar off at the house then race through Sepulveda Pass to Burbank to get to my class at the school by 9:30.

————

It's now Sunday and the kids and I are at a benefit concert to raise money for school music programs in Santa Monica and Malibu. The concert is being held at the Santa Monica High Greek Theater and the featured artist is Jackson Browne. It's a picture-perfect California afternoon with sun and blue skies and a cool ocean breeze that blows against the white canopy covering the outdoor stage. Jonah and I are down on the lawn in the second row. Maddy and her friend Sarah are sitting with Nancy two rows behind us. Nancy and I are getting along again after that showdown over the Therapy Police, mostly because she doesn't seem to remember what happened and because I choose to let it go, knowing what really matters is that I keep things moving along the happy road to our divorce. Even though some members of my family haven't a clue as to why I still socialize with Nancy, I really don't mind these little family get-togethers. Because in this instance, we both love music. And because I know the kids really appreciate the fact that we can still do things together.

During the intermission, just before Jackson comes on, a blond bombshell sits down next to me. There's been no one sitting next to me during the first two acts and now this looker in her thirties arrives with a guy who is clearly much older than her . . . and much uglier than me. He walks off to get drinks and I have trouble keeping my peripheral vision to myself. She seems to be having the same problem. And so, to be polite, I turn to her and say hello. She says hi back and then immediately starts up this conversation about Jackson. I comment on her accent and she tells me she's from the UK. She's in town making a record, her name is Cynthia Evans, she already has a CD out in the States. And she's charming and interesting, and while I keep up with the conversation, I'm thinking to myself, *This is good. This is very good. I'm talking to an attractive woman and my children are close by and it's been a year and a half since I split up with Nancy. And everybody knows Nancy's been seeing someone new. Maybe this is a good way to get the kids used to the idea that someday Dad is going to be with someone new too.*

And that's when the trouble starts.

Maddy suddenly appears and she's standing over us and before I can make introductions, she starts in.

"Dad you need to move your seat." And now I have a situation on my hands. It's called "sabotage." As taught to me by my father, I tell all my classes at the film school to try to find a label for each scene they're either acting in or directing so that they can figure out what the scene is really about. This is the sabotage scene.

I counter by introducing Cynthia to Maddy and Jonah and she seems very happy to meet them and the kids say hi and I'm hoping this will be the icebreaker that'll put an end to any unpleasantness.

"Dad, you need to move your seat right now."

"Maddy, relax, we're just talking."

"No, Dad, you and Jonah need to come sit with Sarah and me right now."

"I don't think so, honey."

But she just stands there, determined, with the sunlight

silhouetting her against an incredibly blue sky. Then Jonah weighs in by whispering in my ear.

"Dad, your talking to that girl is the most disgusting thing I've ever seen."

I can feel the sea breeze blowing in off the Pacific and I take it in just so I can breathe. To breathe and "just sit there." Because the old me wouldn't be breathing and just sitting there, the old me would have lost it immediately by standing up and dragging the two of them off to the side and giving them hell and making a scene right in front of the crowd. The old me would have become totally embarrassed and lost my cool and threatened to take them out of there. The old me would have beaten myself up about the fact that it was a picture-perfect experience until those little brats ruined it. Then again, the old me would have made some excuse to get away from Jonah and run off before the show to take a hit somewhere, then brushed my teeth, chewed on a breath mint, hid my eyes behind my sunglasses and then made it back to my seat, acting as if nothing had happened while my mind was totally fried.

But not today. Not today. "Same family, different day," Shayna, our therapist, would say. Because today, I'm not the same guy. And I just feel too good and I don't want to ruin it. And I'm getting better at doing what I now normally do when confronted with potentially explosive situations: I do nothing. I do absolutely nothing. Because the fact of the matter is, these guys are going to survive. Nancy and I take very good care of them and my children are going to survive quite well. They're simply going to have to get used to the fact that sometimes, and I know this may come as a shocker to the kids, but sometimes, Dad has to take care of . . . Dad.

Maddy's still standing there. Dogged determination. I think

that's why she's such a good student. And then, suddenly, I hear applause and the man of the hour walks onstage and I turn to Maddy.

"Look, honey, it's Jackson Browne. Please go sit down."

And she does.

One of the songs Jackson opens up with is "Take It Easy," the song he wrote for the Eagles. And now I'm thinking this guy's singing to me. Because this alcoholic and addict can be very self-centered, I swear it feels like Jackson's singing to me, he's looking down at me in the second row and he's telling me to Take It Easy.

And the rest of the show is just perfect: Jackson's playing all the hits and the stuff he used to play when I went to his concerts during my college years. Jonah's getting into it, and I turn back to see Maddy, who gives me the thumbs-up. And Cynthia and I manage a little side commentary about the songs until her fat, ugly, gray-haired date shows up.

He's got a wedding ring on. He's got his hand on her knee and she's clearly not comfortable with it. And soon, she gets up and goes off with her VIP pass to watch the show from the side of the stage.

After the show, Nancy and I talk about how great Jackson was. Then I comment on Maddy's behavior.

"Could you believe what Maddy tried to pull?"

Nancy takes a breath, and in a very pregnant reply, like she's happy as hell that Maddy gave me shit, she says, "I know!"

Now I'm driving the kids back to the house. Nancy is meeting a girlfriend for dinner and I'm taking the kids home.

"I mean, I know this is hard for you guys. I know it is. But Mom and I haven't been together for a year and a half and I can't believe you give me crap simply because I'm having a conversation. I know you know Mom has conversations with other guys and she's entitled. And Maddy, I drive you to school every morning and get you there on time, I get you to your tutors, I chaperone your broomball party in the middle of the night, and then I'm driving all your friends home until two in the morning. And this is what I get?"

"Dad, it just grosses us out."

"Yes, Jonah, I understand that, I really do, but I drag you and your surfboard back and forth from the beach, I get you to all your rehearsals, I drag your band equipment to all your gigs, and I really don't deserve to be embarrassed in front of other people just because I'm having a conversation with a woman who happens to be sitting next to me."

I can see that they're starting to feel bad. And frankly, for once, that feels *good*.

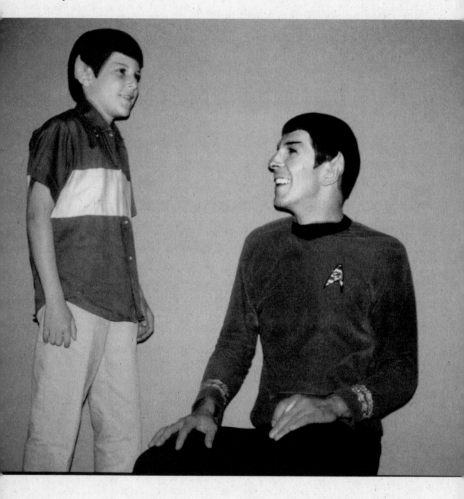

SYNDICATE THIS

WE DIDN'T HAVE a color TV when the series premiered in September '66, and so we all went to a friend's house to watch "The Man Trap," the first aired episode. I like that episode because I had watched some of it being filmed and I remember seeing the salt-sucking monster dummy sitting around on the set, the salt sucker who assumed the human form of a woman named "Nancy." Anyway, we used to watch the show on Thursday nights in my parents' bedroom on their portable black-and-white TV.

Although a TV junkie in the '60s, I didn't watch that much TV during my college years in the '70s, so I wasn't really aware of what was happening with the syndication of the show. I had already been through my Trekkie stage and it was over. One day, my roommate at Berkeley insisted we take a drive down to the Federation Trading Post on Telegraph Avenue. The Federation Trading Post. What a concept. We walked into the store and it was wall-to-wall *Star Trek* paraphernalia. Lots of photos—including the one of me wearing the ears standing on the bridge next to Dad, who's in the captain's chair.

Sure it was fun. They were laughing in the dark. Everyone was gathered around the camera because they knew what was coming, our little surprise for Dad. With all those stage lights pointed at us, after I came onto the bridge and gave Dad, or

Spock, a kiss on his cheek, I looked out to the fourth wall and it was nothing but darkness. Darkness and laughter.

The other thing I really liked about being on the set, besides hanging out with the cast and gazing at Bill Shatner's hairpiece sitting on a mannequin's head in the makeup department, was the smell. Immediately when you walked in it hit you because there was a little room on the stage where these guys made all the little different color knobs you see on the *Enterprise* control panels. They used resin molds to do it. I never sniffed glue to get high, as I was only nine when they started shooting the series, but I loved the smell of model glue as much as the next kid, and this room onstage was a glue sniffer's paradise.

The next inkling that something was going on in the 1970s happened when I was studying with Duncan, a friend of mine, in his dorm room in Cloyne Court, an aging co-op on the north side of the Berkeley campus. We were going through the Plato and Machiavelli and playing Grateful Dead songs on guitar when I stepped out to use the pay phone downstairs to check in with my girlfriend. When I came back, Duncan was gone. In fact, the entire second floor had an eerie silence to it.

I made my way back downstairs. There was a TV room at the end of the hall. The door was ajar and there was a flickering light coming through. I pushed the door open. The room was packed with students. They were all watching a scene where Spock was doing his thing. Someone said to either get in or get out. I looked at Duncan. He gave me a knowing smile. I waved to him and left.

I told Beatrice, my girlfriend, what happened. Beatrice was born in Switzerland. She was pretty and multilingual and knew cool swear words in four languages. She had never seen the show and was curious. And so every weekday at five o'clock, I went up to her house and we watched. And there were three things I rediscovered about that show: (1) some of those *Star Trek* episodes kick ass, (2) Spock rocks!, and (3) I can't remember, probably because I was too stoned at the time, but everything comes in threes so there must have been something else.

And speaking of Spock rocking, I got this call from Justin the other day. He plays bass in a '70s revival band and it's sort of a *Spinal Tap* thing: The guys in the band wear sunglasses and long wigs and big fake mustaches. They play all these classic rock songs and they're a really tight band.

"Dude, our lead singer can't make the gig this Saturday. Do you think your dad would sit in if we offered him seventy-five bucks?"

"Can you guys play 'Proud Mary'?"

"We can play that. We can play anything."

"Well, this might be an interesting way to get his singing career back on track. I'll call him and see what he says."

"Dude, just make sure he knows he has to wear the wig."

ADAM NIMOY
DIRECTOR OF THE YEAR
JULY 23 '95
"OUTER LIMITS"
LOVE, MA

MY MOTHER'S FROM ALASKA

MY MOTHER'S FATHER came from Lithuania and settled in Alaska, where he worked for a fishing cannery. Her mother came from Latvia and settled in Canada. On a trip to Vancouver, my grandparents met, were married, and Archie dragged Ann back to Alaska, where they settled in Cordova, a fishing village where my mom was born. My mom says that's where my grandmother started to lose it—Ann Zoberblatt running around Cordova, looking for a kosher butcher or just another Jewish person for that matter. My mother's name was Sonia, but by the time she came to L.A. and started working in the theater where she met my dad, her name was Sandi Zober. I recently found an old newspaper article about the difficulty census takers were having dealing with driveway gates. It showed a picture of my mom in her early twenties looking over a gate, and the caption read, "Census taker Sandi Sober (sic) trying to gather information."

Mom called me last week because she had some things on her mind.

"Adam, do you ever mention me in your memoirs?"

"What?"

"Do you ever mention me in the memoirs you're writing, because your father never mentioned me. Thirty-two years of marriage and he never bothered to mention me."

"Well, Mom, since you really didn't play that much of a role in my life, I'm not really sure."

My mom starts making these catatonic noises like she's going to have another heart attack over the phone. Sometimes she gets my sarcasm and sometimes she doesn't. But I don't want to make her suffer.

"Mom, of course I mention you; you're all over the memoirs. Every page is saturated with how I couldn't have made it without you."

"Especially my cooking."

Mom's pretty good with the sarcasm herself when she wants to be.

"Yeah, Ma, like your Meat Loaf Surprise and the liver and onions. Makes my mouth water just to think about it."

Mom starts laughing.

"Do you *want* to be mentioned in the memoirs?"

"Well, it would be nice."

"What do you want me to say about you?"

"That I tried so hard to be a good mother. That I tried never to yell at you and I let you get away with stuff sometimes. I stood between you and your father, which may not have been a good thing. I let you have friends stay over and I never made judgments about the friends you ran around with later on except Brian Stevenson, and I never made many judgments about him either. I just tried to be there for you. You would come home from elementary school very angry. The incident with the coat was early on. The gray coat with the elastic neckline. It didn't matter how hot it was, you insisted on wearing that coat. And when the teachers made you take it off, you went bonkers and I had to come get you. You would roll in the grass and then break out, you were so allergic. And I would have to go get you and bring you home. You were a very sensitive kid. It all came from my side of the family of course because we were not *shtarkers*.

"But you were a good boy, a sweet boy. You just got really crazy sometimes. You had a precise world and didn't like it being disturbed. You liked things to be in order. That's why, later on, you started to wash your own sheets and make your bed the way you liked it. And you couldn't stand to have a tag on your shirts. And your shoes had to fit a certain way."

Yeah, my shoes and my shirts and my pants and my underwear . . .

"Now I see you wearing T-shirts and shorts that a few years back you wouldn't walk around in. You just used to look like you stepped out of a band box, a fashion show, your shirts perfectly ironed and your pants perfectly pressed."

I don't know who the hell she's talking about here. Her *other* son maybe.

"Now you come over and you're in a shirt that's not necessarily ironed and shorts. You just don't dress the way you used to. And you tell me your apartment is a mess, but I still have trouble visualizing that. You were always so neat and liked everything to have some sense of order. I guess that shows strides for you. I don't know if it's the therapy or you getting out of an unhappy marriage or what, but *I think you're more comfortable with yourself.*"

HOLLY

I MET HOLLY at a meeting. She's a pretty redhead in her early forties. We're on our first date. We walk down to the beach and sit on the berm overlooking the waves. Holly says that she's been sober six weeks and that she feels like she's finally beginning to live a sober lifestyle. She tells me about her job and how lucky she is to have it and that things are getting exciting because she and her partner are buying out the company. She tells me how great sober sex is. She tells me that when men have sex, they act like they can't believe they're getting laid. They start thinking of other things so as not to come too quickly and so when you look in their eyes and think you're making this big connection, they're thinking about pickle sandwiches or something.

Pickle sandwiches?

She tells me that men are simple, they really want only one thing. She tells me that to keep the sex interesting, you have to stay on the couch as long as possible, because once it gets to the bed, that's where you always go. She tells me that it's better to have sex before going out to eat because afterward, people, especially women, get too full and tired. She happily lets me take the phone calls from my kids as we sit on the beach. She comments that the weather is perfect and it is. She tells me no kissing on the first date but that touching is welcome and then comments that our legs are rubbing up against each other. She keeps touching my arm when she laughs and she laughs a lot.

168

She tells me she was adopted and that she knows she looks like someone, that she never knew her birth mother and is somewhat curious to look her up but is also afraid she'll find her in some run-down trailer park.

———————

When I call her today, she tells me she's disappointed that I can't make the meeting on Monday, that she wanted to look at me knowing that she knows me but not let anyone else know. That she would make eyes at me but not let anyone else see. I tell her how complicated my life is and she tells me that maybe what I need right now is just a friend.

"You mean you want to be 'just friends'?"

"No, I just think that maybe right now, that's what you *need*."

I really like Holly.

We agree to meet in the afternoon on Saturday, July 3, and that I should call her around noon to discuss details. I'm really looking forward to this. On Saturday, I call her at noon and leave a message on her cell. I then drag Jonah and his entire drum kit down to a party in Santa Monica and then I have to run back to the house because he forgot his high-hat stand. When I finally finish with him at one-thirty, I call her again and again it goes straight to voice mail. And then nothing.

And it hit me hard. Because Holly is a no-show. I'm standing in a market getting something to eat when I leave her one last message. And that's the end of that.

And for consolation, I remind myself that she's an addict who hasn't been sober very long and maybe she needs a little more time.

When I talk to her the following week she says she didn't know we had plans and that she was up in Malibu for the day with "a friend."

THE RIV

I'VE SEEN A lot of Spock pix in my day, but one of my favorites is of Dad in full costume and makeup leaning against the front of his first luxury car, a beautiful black Buick Riviera. It's parked in his spot on the Desilu lot directly across from Stage 9, where they shot *Star Trek*. Dad's got his arms crossed and he's got a half-smile going as he leans against the hood of that shiny black car. It's only a black-and-white photo but it's got to be one of the coolest images on the planet.

It was 1966 when he bought the Riv. Dad can be a pretty frugal guy, and he was always very good at living within his means. But *Trek* was on, meaning he had a job for the entire season, meaning he had some money to burn. The Riv was a used '64, but it was beautiful: black with silver trim, pointed leading edges at the front fender, and a sleek contour angled to razor edges at the back. That car looked like the consumer version of the Batmobile, and it was Buick's answer to the Ferrari and the Thunderbird. The Riv didn't so much drive along the streets of Los Angeles as swam. It swam like a killer shark.

Dad enjoyed that car so much that two years later, in 1968, he bought himself a new one. We hadn't had a new car since the Pontiac LeMans that he bought back in '62. The '68 Riviera was brown and it was a tank compared to the Riv and not nearly as cool. But he gave the Riv to my mother and I was glad we kept it in the family.

I really loved the Riv. In fact I loved it so much that in the winter of 1970, when I was fourteen, I would occasionally take it out for a spin in the neighborhood while my parents were out for the evening. This went on for weeks and I got pretty good at driving the Riv until one of my joyrides ended up at the Purdue Police Station in West L.A. where I was mugshotted and fingerprinted along with three girls from my school who were in the car with me.

After my parents bailed me out, I spent the night in a sleeping bag on the floor of their room whimpering and generally feeling sorry for myself. My mother tried to comfort me. My father yelled. He simply didn't know how to deal with this kind of situation. It was an incredibly painful experience. The next day, I was grounded.

———

Oddly enough, the story of the Riv has become an important part of my curriculum at the film school because I'm teaching an acting class now. It's a summer class for high school freshmen students. There are a dozen students in my class out of about a hundred students in the summer program who come from high schools all over the country. I'm giving them "Adam Nimoy's Incredibly Wonderful Lecture on Working with Directors." It's actually the same lecture on acting I'll soon be giving to the directing classes, only then I'll be calling it "Adam Nimoy's Incredibly Wonderful Lecture on Directing Actors." In the lecture, I talk about the practical tools I use on the set to help actors with performance issues. I constantly repeat in all my classes that I teach three things at the film school: story, performance, and the technical aspects of filmmaking, in that order, with strong emphasis on story and performance.

"And when we shoot a show, or a movie, for that matter, we

don't shoot the story in a linear continuum, right? We don't shoot scene one and then scene two and then scene three. We shoot . . . ?"

Someone in the class who knows something about filmmaking answers.

"Out of continuity."

"Yes, we shoot out of continuity. We shoot all the apartment scenes at one time and all the office scenes at one time and all the courtroom scenes at one time. Why is that?"

"Because it's faster."

"Yeah. It's faster and easier and really the only economical way to do it. And because we do so much skipping around, when we're on the set, one of the first things I talk to actors about is where we've been in the story and where we are now so that we're consistent in developing their character arc.

"I do try to schedule story events in order if I can, particularly if I think it's critical to help with performance. But it usually doesn't work that way. Imagine this scenario: A fourteen-year-old boy likes to take his mother's car out for joyrides when his parents are out for the evening. He's not a bad kid but he's looking for some kicks and he grabs a pillow off the living room couch to sit on and takes his mother's luxury car out for a drive through the neighborhood. And after doing this three or four times, he gets cocky one night and picks up three girls who go to his school. And now he's driving on big streets like Westwood Boulevard heading toward the Westwood Village. And while he's stopped at the light at, say, Wilshire Boulevard, who do you think pulls up next to him?"

"His parents."

"Close, and that would make for a funny situation. But no, he's not that lucky and this is not a comedy, it's more of a tragicomedy. Who do you think pulls up right next to him?"

"The cops."

"The cops. And they're looking at this kid and they know he's not sixteen and the girls are telling him to sit up straight and the cops let him drive by and they get behind him and pull him over. And the cops arrest them and handcuff them and drag them down to the police station and separate them and take mugshots of them and fingerprint them. They tell the kid he's going to be charged with driving without a license and stealing a car and reckless endangerment and that he'll probably spend the next six months at a road camp for delinquents. And why do you think they do all this?"

"Because they want to scare him."

"Yeah, they want to scare the shit out of him because the kid's clean, he doesn't have a record. They just want to scare him so he never does it again. And it does scare him. Then his parents come and bail him out and during the car ride home, it's basically the silent treatment because they're going to discuss all this in the morning. And then the next day, we have the 'showdown' scene with the parents, the 'what were you thinking?!' scene where the kid ends up getting grounded. And you're originally scheduled to shoot the police precinct on location. On day three of the production, you're scheduled to shoot the 'scare the shit out of him' scene at an actual police station. The showdown scene with the parents at home shoots on, say, day five, so you're shooting in continuity, which is great, particularly for the actor playing the kid. Why?"

"Because he gets to experience what it's like in the police station."

"Exactly. But guess what? You lose the police precinct because Officer Training Day gets rescheduled to the day you're supposed to shoot and the precinct is no longer available. And now you can't get back in there until day eight, until after the showdown scene with the parents, and you can't move the showdown scene.

"Do you see the problem here? Do you see *your* problem as an actor? Because I would come up to you, the actor, and describe exactly what is going to go down at that precinct. I might go over to the actor playing the kid, and before we rehearse the showdown scene, I might walk him through the whole litany of what went down the night before: the mug shots and the fingerprints and the police in his face and the stuff about road camp and he can hear the girls crying in another jail cell and he barely slept that night after he got home with his parents at one AM. And now rehearsal's up for the showdown scene. I do this kind of thing because I happen to think it's going to help the actor.

"But guess what? That actor may not get that direction. *You* may not get that direction because many directors don't talk to actors either because they don't know how or they just don't have the time. And this is the kind of work you're going to have to do on your own. This is the work of your craft that you need to do to prepare yourself for that showdown scene when, for whatever reason, you aren't given much direction.

One of the girls raises her hand.

"Yes?"

"This sounds like a story about a boy crying for attention."

"Yes, depending on the rest of the story, that may very well be the case, and you can certainly choose to play it that way. Good observation."

But I don't tell her that what the boy really wants is the attention of the girls he picked up that night. I don't tell the class that he wants Sarah and Cyndi and Lori to think he's cool

ADAM NIMOY

so that they'll accept him and bring him into their circle of friends. I don't tell them that although the father is extremely focused on his career, the kid really doesn't want the dad's attention. Because, throughout his childhood, there's been a lot of awkwardness and distance with his father and the kid never intended to put more strain on their relationship.

And I don't tell the class that when the kid turns fifteen and is about to begin driver's training, his mother will laugh out loud when the instructor asks if the kid has any prior driving experience.

MY NEW NOT-SO-BRILLIANT CAREER: EVERYBODY WANTS TO DIRECT

THEY FINALLY ASSIGN me to a one-year directing class. I've had a couple of one-week crash-course directing classes, which went really well, but this is my first time with a full-fledged class. This class is going into its second semester and they're about to start shooting their short films.

The class is a mix of American and international students. I have a guy from Korea, two guys from India, a girl from China, a guy from Italy, a guy from Spain, and a guy from the marines.

When I start with a new class, I try to learn all of their names the first day. I start with the student in the front on the left and ask them to say their name and tell us something about themselves—where they're from, what it's like where they live, and whether they have any experience in film. Then I continue on down the row, always going back to the first student and repeating their names.

"Thank you, Jeff. So that's Cindy and Terry and Barbara and Alex and Cole and Jeff. Next?"

And so on all the way through until I know all twenty-two names. And somehow, I usually manage to remember all of them. I tell them I do this not because I care to learn their names, I do it because I don't want to get Alzheimer's, and scientific studies have proven that memorization is one way to keep senility at bay. But deep down I do it because I know that remembering a student's name is a powerful tool for a teacher because when you call them by name, each and every one of them feels special and gets all warm and fuzzy inside and this helps to get their attention and keep them participating. Except in law school. There you pray the teacher forgets your name.

"So that's Cindy and Terry and Barbara and Alex and Cole and Jeff and Chad and you are?"

"Max."

"Where are you from, Max?"

"Switzerland."

"What part?"

"Zurich."

"Zurich, huh? I had a girlfriend in college who was born in Basel."

"Oh, yes, Basel is very close to Zurich. Just about eighty-five kilometers west."

"I haven't seen her in twenty years. If you happen to bump into her when you get back there, tell her to call me."

"Of course. What's her name?"

"Beatrice. Beatrice McClam. I tried to Google her but she's not very Google-able. So that's Cindy and Terry and Barbara and Alex and Cole and Jeff and Chad and Max and . . ."

"Soren."

"Where are you from?"

"Sweden."

"Any experience in film or TV?"

"I worked for a postproduction company for Norwegian TV shows and I worked for three years as an editor."

"Good, so you have some serious experience. What's life like in Sweden?"

"Cold all the time. July and August are nice summers, the rest of the year it's cold."

"Why do people live there?"

"I don't know. I think it's because of the women. Almost all are blondes."

"Did you leave any Norwegian or Swedish women behind when you left?"

"Ya."

"And were they crying when you left?"

"Ya, all five or six of them. Ya, they were crying."

"Okay, here's the thing, you guys. I know you've already been through directing classes, but I'm going to be reviewing with you some things and then spending class time throughout the semester critiquing your films. In keeping with the curriculum, we teach three things here at the academy: story, performance, and technique, and by that I mean the technical aspect of filmmaking. Now, I know you've spent a lot of time learning all the technical aspects of filmmaking in terms of lighting and camera, and don't get me wrong, that stuff's important. But from my experience working in television, I can tell you that what really matters is story. It's story, folks. Because I don't give a shit how fancy you are with the camera or with lighting or with special effects. If you can't tell a good story, or, more correctly, *show,* because you're working in a visual medium, if you can't show us some little piece of truth about the human condition, then you're wasting your time. Because we have plenty of flashy directors who have wonderful visual style and technique and know all the latest technology. But good storytellers? Those are in very short supply."

That's when Jung Duk Shin walks into class.

"Who are you?"

In a thick accent he answers, "Brian."

"Brian?" I look at the roll sheet. "I don't have a Brian in my class." He tells me in broken English his real name, Jung Duk Shin, which is Korean, but he tells me it's okay to call him Brian.

"I don't like people to be late to my class, Brian. Why are you late?"

He sits down looking bewildered.

"Just for everybody's information, the only excuse I'll accept is if it's because of romance, if it's because of a guy or a girl. Because we can always use a little more love in the world. Why are you late, Brian?"

Alex: "Tell him, Brian. Tell him about the girl."

Jeff: "Tell him, man."

Cindy: "Tell him about your girlfriend, Brian."

Brian sits there like he doesn't have a clue as to what we're talking about.

Brian: "Last night. . . . She was wonderful."

TYPICAL CONVERSATION WITH A TEENAGE DAUGHTER #233: THE WONDERS OF CALL-WAITING

MADDY CALLS ME and she's hysterical because she's just learned from Nancy that I'm not coming over to the house for dinner tomorrow night when the Longs and Lance and Donna are coming over. She's absolutely hysterical.

"Dad, I can't believe you won't do this for me. Why won't you do this, Dad?"

"Because, honey, I have other plans."

Crying and begging and tears.

"But I need you here, Daddy. You have to come. Just say you'll come, say you'll do it for me, Daddy. If you care about me you'll come. Please, Daddy, please!"

"Maddy, you know I care about you, but it's simply not necessary for me to be there. I'm sorry."

Tears and begging and crying.

"Daddy, if you don't come I'm going to kill myself!"

"Oh, Maddy."

"I will, Dad. I will. Why won't you come to dinner? Please. Just for me? Just for me, Daddy, please!"

Begging and tears and crying.

And then a call comes in. I can hear it click in on the line and I know it's for her because I don't have call-waiting. And the next thing I hear is this cool, collected voice.

"Wait, Dad, hold on a minute."

And then she clicks over to the other line.

THE GOOD MOTHER

IT'S THE EARLY 1980s and I'm in law school and I'm going to be an attorney. I'm going to have a steady job and make lots of money. I'm going to be an entertainment attorney and represent big stars. I'll be eating at Morton's or Spago or the Palm or wherever. I'm going to do something my old man can't do. I know what I want and I know where I'm going and I feel sorry for other people who still need to "find themselves."

I found a job. A huge health-care law firm with a small entertainment department. "What's that? I'm going to be working for the litigators before you move me into the entertainment department? Well, I'm really not a litigator but okay, sure. What? You want me to catalog lab reports? You want me to write deposition digests? You want me to draft pleadings? It'll be a year before I join the entertainment department? Oh . . . okay, no problem."

"Every job's an opportunity," Dad would say. I'm just paying dues.

Three years later. I'm looking out the window of my office, looking out on Century City. Every day now I'm looking out wondering what I'm doing here. The partners are nice and I'm working in the entertainment department now, but this is not what I thought it would be: the mountains of paperwork, the phone lists, the staff meetings, the billable hours, the difficult clients, the nasty negotiations. Some people were born for law firm life. I'm pretty sure I wasn't.

"It's important that you feel passionate about your work," Dad would say.

"Hello, Dad? I'm leaving the firm. I'm going to EMI America Records. I'll be in business affairs, which is still legal work but it should be much more fun. I used every connection I had in the music industry to get that job. The competition was fierce. I want to be in music. That's where my passion is."

EMI America! I love this job! The zany people, the concerts, the merchandising, the art department, the bands. I met David Bowie! Yeah, there's still plenty of paperwork but I *love* this job. I really love this job.

Absolutely certain where I'm going.

"Back-to-back hits with *Star Trek IV* and *Three Men and a Baby*? Way to go, Dad. You're still out of town? I gotta read you this article in the *L.A. Times*. It says you're the common link between those two movies. You're the reason that they're hits. Way to go!"

My parents are getting divorced. I'm thirty and old enough to know it's been coming for some time. Ironically, Dad's in Toronto working on *The Good Mother,* about a woman fighting for the custody of her daughter.

I'm on the phone with him while he's in Toronto.

"Dad, it's over at EMI. I know it's only been a year but they haven't had any hits and they're merging the company and I'm out. Maybe I should have seen it coming. There's not much happening right now. Tommy Werman got me an interview at Polygram and it went really well. But I just talked to him and his sources at the company say I'm not black enough. I don't know if that's an excuse or what.

"I'm looking at the music publishers and the other major

labels and I'm working part-time for another firm, but they don't have a full-time position. I'm interviewing at the talent agencies and even thinking about production. I need to look for other things and keep all options open because there are simply too many attorneys in this town looking for work."

The response from Toronto is neither encouraging nor helpful. Here's my side of the conversation:

"That is so untrue. I followed up on every lead you gave me."

"Dad, he wasn't looking for me and I wasn't looking for him."

"Trust me, it was the wrong situation. If I'm going to work for an independent producer, we have to click and we didn't. That was clear to both of us."

Over the phone, I can hear the sound of ice hitting the glass.

"Nothing I say is ever good enough, so what's the point."

"Yeah, I know I told you agencies were out of the question, but I'm looking for a job. It's so tight out there right now I have to consider all the possibilities."

"That is not what I said, and when you start in like this, you're not being helpful."

"Oh, yeah, okay, Dad, you just keep swinging. That's right, give it the ole one-two. Enough of the left jab, just go for the knockout with your right. In fact, I'm on the canvas now, so why not just go for the kick in the face to finish the job."

"Stand up and take it? You've got the wrong guy. I think you're just being mean because you're so miserable. You are so incredibly miserable and I feel sorry for you."

"Because you're obviously in so much pain."

"Oh, Dad. I don't think so. Just look at yourself. I don't think I've ever seen you this miserable."

GOT RAGE?

I'M A SUCKER for Horatio Alger stories—where any member of society can achieve the American Dream of wealth and success through hard work, courage, and determination. That's why I love the stories about where Dad came from, born in Boston of Russian Jewish parents who scrimped and saved to provide for their two sons. Max, his father, was a barber. Dora, his mother was frugal. They lived in a Jewish-Italian tenement in the West End of Boston. During the Depression, Dad sold newspapers in Boston Common. As a teen, he sold vacuum cleaners and life insurance. I still remember the early '60s when, between acting jobs, Dad had a business servicing office fish tanks. He also had a route of gumball machines, worked in a pet store, and managed an apartment building in Venice where some of the tenants pretended to be out when he came to collect the rent. I remember all these things because they remind me of where we came from. But I never had to work those kinds of jobs and the differences in our upbringings laid the cornerstone for the conflict that was to come.

"You both have a problem," Bernie Francis, Dad's business manager of forty-plus years used to say. "His is in understanding you, yours is in getting through to him."

Dad and I came from different worlds, or planets, so sometimes it was very difficult for us to communicate—especially about sensitive subjects. My father grew up in a household where talking about your feelings was not a top priority. And his celebrity only made matters worse. Since the beginning, people have been coming up to Dad from every direction wanting something, whether it was an autograph, or to have a picture taken with him, or to get an endorsement or maybe a contribution. Naturally, Dad had to be very guarded when dealing with these types of situations and oftentimes, he forgot to let his guard down when relating to me.

By the time I was a teenager, the combination of dealing with the usual issues of school and socializing, and a celebrity dad who had trouble differentiating my needs from those of the fans brought on an acute sense of frustration, even rage. And then there was the acting out that comes with rage, like stealing the Riv, fighting with my sister, and running with a fast crowd who taught me how to drink and take drugs.

But Mom was paying attention. So she sent me to therapy.

Jack had games in his office. Week after week we played cards and checkers and pickup sticks. *The man knew how to play.* Jack was like Judd Hirsch in *Ordinary People*—for the first time an adult male took an interest in my thoughts and feelings. The fact that he was paid to was not terribly relevant. And after three months of playing games, we finally got down to business. The rage got better but it was still there—along with an ever-widening black hole. Sure, I had a better understanding of why Dad did the things he did: his disapproving mother, the competition with his brother the college graduate, being raised in the Depression, the obsession with his career and generating income just to survive. Jack helped me figure it out. But that's all intellectual. Just because I'm smart enough to understand doesn't mean I can just let go of everything— everything that happened or didn't happen, everything that he said or didn't say, everything that's in my hard drive. In this case, unlike Paula's "Feelings are not Facts" it's more like "Facts are not feelings"—just because I have the facts straight doesn't mean my feelings are going to automatically fall in line. For that, I'm now convinced, I also needed the tools of 12-Step recovery. And during most of my adult life, I simply didn't have those tools. And so the hole got bigger. Enter drugs and alcohol to fill the hole and that's how I coped. "Self-medicating" the therapists call it. But that kind of self-help goes only so far. Because rage combined with the drugs and alcohol and the pressure cooker of working in Hollywood created an awful lot of trouble on the set. When the producers would start making demands and pushing my buttons, my insides would start bubbling and I would just want to kill somebody. I was one big walking emotion ready to react at any given moment. Not unlike what my daughter feels when she writes me hate e-mails or tries to grab my steering wheel to make a point. Except she was fourteen. I was forty.

I did have many outstanding experiences in TV, and I produced a lot of work that I'm very proud of, not the least of which was the episode of *The Outer Limits* I directed, with Dad in the starring role. But there were a few too many crashes.

Remember Terrence Howard, who played a TV director in the film *Crash*? There's a scene in that film where white-bread Tony Danza, who plays a TV producer, starts to lecture Terrence on how to direct black actors, that one of the actors in the scene Terrence just directed was talking "less black" than he should be. Terrence just laughs it off but Tony challenges him by asking, "Is there a problem?" Then they cut to a close-up of Terrence, and you know what's going through his mind, because of all the things that happened to him in the movie, you know he's thinking: *"Fuck you, white honky."* You can see it in his eyes. And you're wondering, *What's he gonna do?*

What's he gonna do? What's he gonna do? But then he gets a grip and his mouth says, "No, we don't have a problem," and they go back for another take.

That's where Terrence is a better man than I, because a TV show is not the place to go toe-to-toe with the producer. It's the producer's show, not the director's. It's Tony's show, not Terrence's. Freelance TV directors are just hired guns for that episode, and then we leave to go to another show. That's why Terrence is a better man than I. At least in that situation, he controlled his rage—only to let it fly later in the movie. Quite often, I didn't have that control. When that happened to me, when a producer came over to put the squeeze on me and tell me what to do, and I happened to think that he was full of shit, more often than not my mind was thinking, *Fuck you, white honky*, and my mouth was saying, "Fuck you . . . white honky."

And after I told him to stick it, the producer would pull me off the set and inform me that I was shooting myself in the foot. And when I finished directing those shows, after I had shot one or both of my feet off, I would hobble home, pull my bottle of Canadian Club off the shelf, grab my bong, go out back, and proceed to finish the job by blowing my head off.

THE NEVER-ACTUALLY-TAPED
DICK CAVETT INTERVIEW

SOMETIMES I HAVE this fantasy that Dad and I are on *The Dick Cavett Show* from the '70s—only it's taking place in the present. It's "Celebrity Father and His Wayward Son" interview night and we're talking about all kinds of things, like the night Dad hung out with Jimi Hendrix in Cleveland, the reasons why he decided to become an actor, and how I switched from the law to directing. And the conflict. We're talking about the conflict and the differences between us. And Dad is saying things, things I want to hear, things I *need* to hear.

Here's what it looks like without the commercials:

DICK: Adam, you talked earlier about the generation gap and the difficulties you and your dad had with each other when you were growing up and when you were out of work.

ADAM: Well, yeah, I think it's sometimes difficult because, in a way, Dad never really had a childhood. He had to grow up pretty fast just as a matter of survival. He's the son of immigrant parents who ended up in Boston and he was raised during the Depression, so from early on, he was extremely focused on work and generating income. But being raised in sunny Southern California in an affluent family was a totally different experience, and although I really admire Dad's work ethic and have tried very hard to emulate it, sometimes I think that the huge difference in our experiences created obstacles between us that we've both had to work very hard to overcome.

DICK: Leonard, would you say that's a fair assessment?

LEONARD: I think Adam's right. I was raised a certain way with a certain attitude and mind-set. When I came to Hollywood, it took me eleven years of supplementing my acting income with odd jobs before I was able to support myself in my profession. Once things started happening and I was actually getting somewhere, I was pretty much focused on staying on the train and keeping the ride going.

DICK: The train meaning the trajectory of your career.

LEONARD: Yeah, it's been my experience in Hollywood that you need to spend a lot of time and energy trying to break through, which is probably true in any profession. But acting jobs can be over fairly quickly and your career can fizzle out very fast. So you're constantly looking for work to stay in the game and it can really drive you crazy. Remember, we were only on *Star Trek* for three seasons.

DICK: I was always under the impression that it was much longer than that, like thirty seasons, maybe.

LEONARD: Seventy-nine episodes were all we made so I really had no time to relax and feel safe that I had "arrived." I felt compelled to keep feeding the monster as well as finding new ways to supplement my income through personal appearances and recordings and conventions and theater work. And unfortunately, all of that does take away from focusing on family time and family issues, issues that I was not necessarily capable of addressing. So in that respect, my work was an escape. It may very well have been my obsessive need to keep working and my fear of not having enough work that made me nervous about the times Adam was out looking for jobs and considering other career avenues after he put so much time and effort into his law career. . . .

———————

"Okay, Dad, I think I'm going to hang up now."

"Dad . . ."

"Dad! Can I get a word in edgewise?"

"Just let me say a sentence."

"If you don't stop yelling I'll have no choice but to hang up."

"Now, I'm doing the best I can in a very unfortunate situation. I'm considering all possibilities, yes, including getting on a desk working for an agent or getting into film or television development. Just be patient. Something will turn up."

Something did turn up. I received an offer from Enigma Records to join the Business Affairs department doing what I did at EMI. It was another great gig and I was back on track to where I thought I was going. Except that three years later, with no major hit records, the company disappeared and I was back on the street.

Maybe I should have seen it coming. One thing was for sure: My passion for my chosen career was fading.

———————

DICK: Leonard, Hollywood is full of stories of people who come from nowhere and make it big and even more where people come to Hollywood looking for fame and fortune and never find it. Such as myself. I'm wondering what your perception is of all that in terms of your story.

LEONARD: The fact is, I can see now that if it weren't for the role of Spock coupled with the huge success of the syndication market, a lot of opportunity, in terms of the movies and so forth, might not have come my way. Don't misunderstand me: When *Star Trek* and *Mission: Impossible* were over, I worked very hard at my craft, doing stage work and branching out into photography and other TV fare like *In Search of . . .* I was driven to succeed and I think Adam has a similar mind-set. But a lot of what happens in Hollywood also has to do with luck and circumstance.

DICK: With all that in mind, how receptive were you to the idea of Adam switching professions and trying to follow in your directing footsteps?

LEONARD: I was very supportive. I did have some concerns, because I was very excited when he became a lawyer. But I could also see why he wanted to make the change and I was proud of that fact that he wanted to follow in my footsteps. And it just so happened we were making *Star Trek VI* at the time and so I brought him on board to learn about the process, and when that project wrapped I suggested he talk to Rick Berman on *The Next Generation*. And that's where he got his first directing job.

ADAM: The whole idea of switching actually started in Jeff Corey's acting class. Jeff was an old friend of the family. In fact, Dad took over Jeff's acting classes in the early sixties when the blacklist was over and Jeff started working again. Wasn't it nineteen sixty-two, Dad?

LEONARD: I think it was in sixty-three.

ADAM: And wasn't that where your students put up a production of *Oedipus Rex*?

LEONARD: Yes, it was.

ADAM: And didn't I have to leave the theater because I thought I was going to throw up when Milt Cohen came out onstage with blood dripping from his eyes?

LEONARD: (Smiling) Yes, you did.

ADAM: Anyway, Jeff was a terrific actor and when I was in between jobs at EMI and Enigma, he invited me to come out to his actor's workshop. And the very first day I went out there, I was in total shock: There were about fifteen students mostly in their twenties. And the scene work and the monologues were incredible. What really impressed me was how Jeff was able to coax performances out of his students, and that was it—I was hooked. I had goose bumps on my arms during the entire class and that's when I started to think I was in the wrong profession. I became a student in that class for almost two years, not because I was interested in acting, it was the directing, the way Jeff communicated with the actors that fascinated me. I didn't dump the law career right away because, as Dad said, I had invested a lot of time and effort into that career, but when it was over at Enigma, I was ready.

"It won't be long, Dad. I'll be making movies just like you. It won't be long. I won't be in TV very long." But after eleven television seasons and forty-five episodes, my addictions and my personality and my marital problems all caught up with me and it was over: "They never complain about the work," my agent would say, "just the attitude."

"Yes, Dad, I know you put out a lot of effort and opened a lot of doors for me and I screwed it up. You're right and I'm sorry. What else do you want me to say?"

"Yes, all true, but must you accentuate the negative?"

ADAM: Sometimes, I would get so frustrated trying to break through to him, trying to explain that I'm not built like him, that we're not all so talented or so lucky or so frugal and some of us have to struggle more than others. I mean, it's like I can't get him to see the logic and it really gets infuriating sometimes and my rage kicks in and I just want to grab him by the shoulders and shake him and yell, "DAD, WHAT PLANET ARE YOU ON?!"

The thing is, in struggling to follow in Dad's footsteps, I knew I had the passion for the work, just like Dad, I knew I had it. And Jeff's acting class and the other filmmaking classes I took taught me the craft. But did I have all that it takes to succeed? "The entertainment business is not a meritocracy," Dad would say, meaning that success in the business doesn't rely solely on talent. I now know that people who seem to have lesser skills have passed me by because of circumstance or because they have other talents that I do not possess. But when I look back on my directing experience as a whole I'm happy with what I've achieved and thankful for the opportunities given to me.

LEONARD: I think in the long run, I've been very lucky in my work and in the opportunities that have presented themselves to me. I've tried to teach Adam as much as I could, and I think he has struggled very hard to get to where he is. He's in a good place now where he feels passionate about his work, about his teaching, although it might not have been what he wanted or expected in the first place.

THE BONER KING

ON TUESDAY, I get an e-mail from Holly. I've been seeing her at the Monday night meeting and I still enjoy talking to her even though she dumped me on July 3rd for Steven, the guy she's now dating. She says she knows we're "just friends" but wants to know if I'll go with her to a birthday party on Friday night. Turns out she's having "issues" with Steven and he's going to be out of town. The party's at a house on the beach in Malibu. She says she promises it'll be "purely plutonic." She says she just wants to go with a sober buddy. So I write back that I would love to go as long as it's "plutonic." I tell her that if it were "platonic," I would've passed because the idea of going without at least the possibility of sex doesn't really appeal to me. I also tell her I first have to go to an early screening of some short films at the film school but I should be back in time for the party. She writes back with a "Yippee!" and signs off with two xx's.

It's Friday night and I'm wading through traffic trying to get to the screening on time. We're screening two short films made by the producing class. I'm their directing instructor so it's important that I be on time, especially because I always lock the door at the beginning of class and stick it to them for being even a minute late. Despite my best efforts, I arrive late and—ha, ha—the students have locked me out of the screening room and when they let me in they stick it to me.

We get started immediately. Ron, the producing instructor, insists I say a few words and refuses to let me pawn it off on him. I wasn't prepared for this so I give them the usual bullshit that I happen to totally believe in: about how this is a collaborative art form and that the students are lucky to be able to see the production process from a number of different perspectives. Because good producers also know a lot about writing and directing and you need these skills to be competitive in this business and thank you for letting me be a part of the process. And we watch the movies. And they're not half bad.

Afterward, I try to make a quick getaway to Holly and the beach party, but one of the students comes up and says he wants to get some one-on-one instruction from me. I keep thinking he's saying some "101" instruction, and at first I don't know what the hell he's talking about. And the dean told him to talk to me, and if I was okay about it, we could work something out through the school. And when I finally figure out what he's talking about, my mind starts racing. Because I really like this kid but I'm thinking this is going to cost him big-time because I'm pretty sure he didn't hear a fucking thing I said in class. I mean, I actually really like this kid but I just want to get going and I can't stop my mind from racing:

Every time I looked over at you in class, you were looking out the window or at the floor or at your dick. And you never wrote a single thing I said down on paper and it's no fucking wonder you had reshoots on your movie and when we were in production, you wore your lucky 'Boner King' T-shirt that's laid out in the Burger King logo. And you may be the Boner King but you did not follow your shot list and you looked pretty impotent during the shoot and that is why if you get any personal '101' instruction from me, it's gonna cost you big-time.

That is what's racing through my mind. But my recovery

seems to be working because my mouth keeps saying, "Sure thing. Whenever you're ready. Just let me know."

I finally ditch the Boner King and drive like hell to that party in Malibu. Gotta get there before Holly takes a drink. And she's there waiting for me in a low-cut blouse and black slacks. And I'm not too late. And she's so damn pretty that I have to remind myself again that she's dating someone else and that she hasn't had much time in sobriety. And the house on the beach is big and expensive. The decor consists of black leather furniture and flat-screen TVs. The guest room looks like a teenage girl used to live there years ago and now she's in college but nothing in her room has been touched, including the tattered white shag carpet, the collection of little perfumes, and the stuffed animals that sit waiting on her bed. Except there is no teenage daughter who's in college. Holly explains there's only her friend the bachelor attorney who bought the place five years ago fully furnished, so the teenage girl's bedroom is really not his fault. I'm thinking, *He's been here five years and hasn't touched the teenage daughter's bedroom, the teenage daughter from another fucking family?*

But I didn't make a big deal about it because Holly looks so hot tonight. I can feel the heat.

There are a bunch of youngsters at the party because it's a birthday party for some guy who's turning thirty, a guy Holly doesn't even really know. There's a looker, a blonde in a halter top and blue jeans, and she keeps looking at me but I can't figure out if she's interested or just wondering what a middle-aged man is doing at this party. There are about six servers in black tie, which is a lot of help for a party of maybe twenty-five. And the finger foods are from Costco. And Lawrence, the lawyer who owns this place, looks about as old as me even though he's ten years younger. I guess the law can do that to you. Holly tells me he's a recreational coke user. I guess coke and the law can do that to you. As it happens, Lawrence and I went to the same law school, and when I tell him the year I graduated, all he can say is, "My, you *are* old."

The blonde keeps looking me over but I can't get to her and she's too young anyway. And Holly's mind seems to be racing like she needs a drink or a fix, but that's why I'm here because I'm her only sober friend right now and she wants me there because she wants to be with me and she wants me to keep her sober and she wants me to meet her nonsober friends. After about an hour and a half, I'm starting to wonder what the hell I'm doing here. People are constantly going in and out of the bathroom and I just know there's blow in there. I can smell it.

So I go to the bar but there's no one tending because the bartender's off in the corner sweet-talking a cute server. I fix myself a soda and lime. Holly comes up and, for some reason, asks if I'd like a water bottle. With my drink in hand, I say sure, and as I watch her walk off with her tight figure to the kitchen, I can't help but think about what it would be like to take her down. And now I am so fucking frustrated, I am so sexually frustrated because I really want that girl. I want her *now*. But I have to remind myself again that I'm just here to help her stay sober and to meet her friends and to watch her dance as her body sways and her hips move to the hip-hop beat.

I meet her friends. Two of them work with her at the agency and one works with Larry at the law office. I meet her friend Rebecca, who's got a little something going with her blue jeans and cool black leather jacket and black sandals. Rebecca's nice and we have this great conversation that I really need right about now to keep me at this party where it's torture to be around Holly and I don't know anyone else here and there's nothing to eat and the blonde keeps looking at me but there's no way to get to her. Rebecca and I sit and talk for almost half an hour while we silently wonder what it would be like to fuck each other. She finally gets up to powder her nose, and I tell Holly I don't know how much longer I can stay and is she going to be all right without me or should I take her home. She says it's not a problem, not to worry, that her friends will take care of her. She asks me if I asked Rebecca for her number and I say no, I wanted to ask her first if it was okay, and Holly says that she's not sure, that it might be hard for her if I did.

Then she puts her arms around me and holds me in the middle of the party. She holds me close as if we're all alone. I can feel her perfect body tight against my not-so-perfect body. I'm getting turned on, totally turned on, I just want to jump out of my skin. And I have to focus on breathing to calm myself down and to keep from making a fool of myself.

Then a stupid thought comes to mind: I start thinking that the Boner King has nothing on me. Because I bet I'm just as horny as he is, even though he's twenty-something and I'm . . . well, as Lawrence the lawyer says, I'm old. And we're holding each other tight and moving to the beat, right in the middle of the party, on the dance floor, with people looking on, with Rebecca and the pretty blonde looking on. But I don't care about them, I just want to hold Holly and pretend she's mine, pretend that we're together and that we were in bed all night and that I gave her everything I had.

The song finally ends.

"I don't know, Adam. There's something about you that gets me, I don't know, that gets me a little crazy, I guess. I don't know what it is."

"I know. Believe me, I'm feeling the same way. But we have to wait. You need to hold on a little longer."

"Why?"

"Because, Holly, you really don't have enough time. And you're still with Steven anyway and you really should be dealing with your issues with him."

Holly nods in agreement as she begins to loosen her hold on me. Without the drink or the drugs I'm feeling so much inside right now that I'm suffocating and have to get out of there.

"I have to go. Are you sure you're going to be okay if I leave?"

"The girls will watch out for me."

She walks me to the door. I give her a hug and she lightly kisses me.

As I walk down the stairs to the boardwalk on the beach, I look back to see her waving and smiling from the balcony. I am so relieved to get the hell out of there and the ocean night air cools me down. And then I start thinking that we're not so very different, the Boner King and I, that I'm just as impotent because I can't go home with Rebecca, because I couldn't get to the pretty blonde, because I can't be with Holly.

And when I get back to my car, there's a forty-seven-dollar parking ticket waiting for me on my windshield.

BIANCA

BIANCA WAS A BLIND date. Luckily, she turned out to be pretty. And smart. And we have some things in common: She's a Hollywood brat like me with some of the attendant issues and she's divorced with two kids.

It started on her couch. It was our second date. She invited me over while her kids were at their dad's place. We were talking and then she kissed me. Then I kissed her back, and then she asked me back, night after night, even if her kids were there. But they didn't know about me. She was worried it was too soon for me to meet them. I didn't argue. She'd put them to bed and I'd stand outside her front door waiting. Waiting like I used to do when my dealer wasn't home yet—waiting outside and jonesing for a fix. No, with much gratitude, I can say I wasn't a junkie, I wasn't a pill head, I wasn't a coke- or crackhead. But I would be jonesing for Mary Jane anyway.

Yes, Bianca was pretty and smart and easy to be with. And when her ex had the kids, I would sleep at her house and she made it all very comfortable for me: I would wake up next to her in the morning with the sun and the lace curtains and the white sheets. And her.

And in bed she would ask me trick questions like: "Would you ever tell me how to dress?"

"Why would I? You have some very pretty things in your closet."

"Because this guy I dated once tried to dress me."

"That's ridiculous."

And then one night, while we were in each other's arms: "Have you ever lied to me? Wait, you don't have to answer that."

"Bianca, I have never lied to you," I said as my eye twitched uncontrollably.

For my birthday, she took the time to make me two CDs of her favorite music. It was sweet. I really felt her affection, although in keeping with good form, we never used the *L* word.

Back in Carol's office again. The licensed social worker.

Me: "She uses phrases like 'Indeed, I did' and 'I suppose.'"

Carol: "With all the things you seem to like about her, those words might be something you can live with."

Me: "I suppose."

———

Okay, I think I'm in love with Bianca. She's so nice to look at and she's well read and has taste and style and it just feels right to be with her. She treats me like I'm something special. Just the way she said good-bye to me yesterday. I held her tight and then watched her go down the stairs and she was just perfect with her petite figure, her long, flowing black hair, and her freckled shoulders. And just before she was out of sight, she turned and smiled. And I was so glad to have waited at the top of the stairs to see her smile. Okay. I think I'm in love with her.

There's nothing like lying on the beach holding a girl you're in love with while feeling the sun and the wind and hearing the ocean's roar. Looking into those green eyes and stretching your arm out with a camera to take your picture together as though you really are together, as though you're really an item.

But that was in August.

Now it's September and I think she's screwing with me. For some reason, I've suddenly become low priority on her activity list. The e-mails have stopped coming and the invitations to come-over-at-a-moment's-notice have stopped. We make plans and then she cancels at the last minute because she has to go to the opera or she forgot she has to watch the Emmy Awards or she has to fly to Vegas. And when she says, "Call me tonight," and I do, she doesn't answer her cell phone and doesn't return my calls. Now I have to pull away and protect myself. It's been a while since I was dumped: I almost forgot how it feels. Being stood up by Holly on that second date was nothing compared to this.

And now she doesn't answer my e-mails. And I have to wonder, Why? *Why?* What happened? After two weeks of this nonsense, I think I've had enough, so I withdraw to protect myself. I'm really not sure what else to do, it's been so long.

The Emmy Awards. She stood me up for Bill Shatner's big night at the Emmy Awards.

THE SPACE TO CRY

AS PART OF MY AA literature commitment, I'm supposed to
bring directories to the Monday night meeting. The directories
have schedules of all the AA meetings in town, and I think
they're really important for people who need to find another
meeting. But I'm out of them and I didn't have time this week
to go to the central office to buy more. I have some directories stashed at Chris Kelton's house for our Thursday night
meeting, so I drive over to pick them up. I have Maddy in the
car because I just picked her up from Becca's house in Santa
Monica.

We pull up to Chris's house. The old Lincoln and the older
Chevy Malibu are in the driveway.

"Maddy, are you coming in with me?"

"I don't know if I should. Is James there?"

"Honey, I have no idea."

"I'm not sure whether or not I should come in."

"I'm just going in to pick up some books. I'll be right
back."

She stays in the car. I go inside and Chris is there and I dig
through his closet and pull out the directories. As I'm about to
leave, James appears.

"Hey, James, how's it going?"

"All right."

"Good to see you. Gotta run. Chris, I'll see you on Thursday."

I walk back to my car.

"Was James there?"

"Yeah."

"Why didn't you have him come out to say hi to me?"

I didn't see this coming, so I get a little defensive.

"Maddy, I didn't know you wanted him to come out to say hi."

Now she starts to lose it.

"What do you think, Dad? You should have told him to come say hi to me."

Now she starts to cry.

"Why didn't you tell me to come in? Why didn't you tell me, Dad? Why didn't you?"

"Maddy, honey, I didn't know you wanted to come in that badly. I didn't know James was going to be there. You've had this love-hate thing with him forever and I didn't know."

"You should have told me to come in. You should have told him to come out."

Now she's really a mess, and I'm at a total loss.

"Maddy, if I had known, I would have asked him to come out. Why don't we go back and I'll take you inside."

The tears are streaming.

"What's the point, Dad? He'll know we just came back so I could see him. I can't believe you did that. I just can't believe it."

"I can't read your mind, honey. I want to do things for you, you know I do, but I can't read your mind. I wish you had told me, I feel so bad. I don't know what to do."

I know it's not just about James. I mean, yes, it *is* about James. But it's also about all the other things going on in her

life: she just started school again and she has to go from Spanish to gym to English to math to history to chemistry and she's
just getting used to the schedule and she's tired. And I know
she's crying because her parents are getting divorced, and I'm
not around as much as I used to be because she still refuses
to stay at my apartment. We used to make the best dinners together and while we were eating I'd always say, "Well, Maddy,
we did it again." Or at night, I'd sit nearby and read a book
while she did her homework.

I miss that so much. I ache for it.

And now there's absolutely nothing between my feelings
and me—ever.

Sometimes I hate feeling my feelings.

It's times like these when I think I'm just like them, I'm just
like those mothers who get up at the meetings and talk about
how their alcoholism and their addiction caused them to lose
their children. I always used to think, *Thank God that's not
me.* But it's times like these and when I go home alone at night,
when I go home and my children aren't there, when I can't go
in their rooms at the house while they're asleep to just sit and
look at them then get up and give them kisses that don't wake
them, it's times like these that I feel like I'm just like those
mothers, that I've lost my children.

I know Maddy misses me and all the things I used to do for
her and with her. *I know it.* And I know she's crying because
of all these things and still other things that go on with fifteen-
year-old girls that I don't even know about. And I know she's
crying because of James.

So I let her cry. As I drive her back to the house, as we pass
my old run-down house on Palms Boulevard, I just give her the
space to cry.

———

The following week, I'm going to the Thursday night meeting. Maddy says she's coming with me to watch *The O.C.* with James while we have the meeting. And everything goes beautifully. When I take her home, I turn to her and say, "I am so glad you got the chance to be with James and fix that little problem we had last week."

"Yep, so am I. It was really nice. It's really nice just hanging out with him."

And then I do it again. While I'm driving, I reach over and squeeze her knee. And with the intensity of love, I say to her, gritting my teeth as I keep squeezing, "You've got knees, Maddy. You've got the knees in the family!"

THE THIRTEENTH STEP

BACK TO THE Monday night meeting: dirty white linoleum, oppressive fluorescents, uncomfortable brown fold-out chairs, bad coffee, cheap cookies. I'm ten minutes early, so I get a cup of tea and take a seat as the room starts to fill.

Holly walks in and sits down next to me. Now that there's trouble with Bianca, I'm having a hard time keeping my mind off Holly. The addict's way: gotta fill that big black hole in my life with something other than drugs or alcohol, whether it's sex or money or love or chocolate. Or recovery. I have to remind myself that trouble with Bianca does not equal sex with Holly.

Then there's the fact that she's still with the guy she stood me up for back in July.

"I broke up with that guy."

"Steven? I thought you were going to try to work through your issues with him."

"Yeah, well, it just wasn't working out. He's too distracted by his kids and his job, and he's really just a nerd who knows nothing about music and never took drugs, and it just seems so hard to find someone who has a background in music and is solid but still has a spark."

"You mean like me?"

"Yes, Adam, like you."

Holly squeezes my arm and laughs. I can't help but smile back at her as the room starts to fill up.

"Anyway, I just wasn't a priority. I mean, I'd call him and he wouldn't call back right away and that just drives me nuts."

"Like, how long would he take to call back?"

"Sometimes he'd call me the next day and that was too hard for me. I have too many needs, and when he's not with his kids I expect him to be with me all the time, but he runs a business and has other things on his mind. And sometimes, when I'm with him, I have no idea where his mind is. I don't know . . . Enough about me. What about you? How are you doing?"

"Well, I may be breaking up with someone tonight."

"Really? I didn't know you found someone. You said you weren't ready."

"No, Holly, I said *you* weren't ready because you were a newcomer and you still are."

"I know. You're right."

"And, you stood me up on July third."

"Oh, my God, Adam, that again? You mean *we* should've taken that hotel room in Malibu?"

"Yeah, if you hadn't blown me off for Steven, things might be different."

"I wasn't with Steven."

"Yes, you were, Holly. You told me yourself. You told me he, quote, 'whisked you away up the coast for the day.'"

"Oh, yeah. I remember. How long have you been seeing this girl?"

"A couple of months."

"Does she have kids?"

"Yeah."

"Where'd you meet her, PTA?"

"No, but that's very funny. Blind date."

"And how's the sex?"

This girl is killing me. I mean, I love it that she's so forward because no woman I know talks like that and it's a total turn-on, as are her tight brown corduroys and her low-cut orange sweater. She's sexy and provocative—in a good way—and she doesn't seem to care that it's close to meeting time and the place is filling up. There's Aaron, who likes to put his leg around Holly when he hugs her hello, and there's Ryan, who told her he'd crawl a mile on his hands and knees "just to get a peek." *Just to get a peek.* Such dogs. But so am I because her low-cut sweater keeps screaming for my eyes. I have to fight to keep from looking down. She has gorgeous long red hair that's pulled back in a ponytail.

I've never been with a redhead.

"So how is it with her?"

"You don't beat around the bush, do you?"

"There are certain things I want to know right away. So how is it?"

"Oh, God, Holly, I don't know, the sex is, it's . . . it's good. I mean, what can I say, she's a little bit conservative, as are most of the women I've been with, but I still really enjoy being with her. I bet *you're* not terribly inhibited."

"No way. I get crazy. Sometimes it gets to be too much, but I draw the line at animals."

"That's comforting."

"So what happened with this girl?"

"Oh, her attitude started to change and suddenly I became a low priority in her busy world."

"Sounds vaguely familiar. So what are you going to do?"

"I'm not really sure. I've got to call her tonight and deal with it."

"If it doesn't work out, will you call me?"

"You're terrible."

"I know, I'm sorry, I didn't really mean it. I mean, I did, but I want it to work out for you. I mean, I don't. I mean, I *do* want you to be happy, you know that."

"I know and I want the same for you."

"So, then, will you call me?"

"You'll be my rebound girl."

"We can be each other's rebound."

"My sponsor would kill me. He's sitting right behind you, you know."

She turns around to look. Mitchell's back there: big, burly, black glasses, always looks like he needs a shave. He's sitting back there with Justin. Justin's with a pretty brunette I don't recognize. The two boys beam funny smiles and wave at us.

"Him? He's the guy who told you not to have sex with me?"

"Him and Justin and a half dozen other people. Holly, it's the thirteenth step: *No dating newcomers*. You've only been sober what, four months?"

"Five."

"Five months is good but it's not very long, and you talk about your sober sex life, but you're really still in withdrawal and you're substituting sex for drugs."

"Oh, really? And what about you?"

"I've been sober for two years, and I'm still in withdrawal and I'm substituting sex for drugs."

ALL I WANT IS THE TRUTH

I CALLED BIANCA that night and I was right: It's over. I haven't been dumped in a long time but now I remember: It doesn't feel good.

I have to come up with something to read at Beyond Baroque in Venice for the end of this cycle in my writer's workshop. All the classes come together and everyone gets a chance to read, but because there are so many of us, we each have only two minutes. After two minutes Jack blows the fart whistle, and if there isn't an immediate wrap-up, the water pistols come out. I want to write something about Bianca without laying too much blame. As per Mitchell, I've got to take my own inventory to see what role I played in this latest crash and burn. I've been writing the Bianca piece all week, paring it down line by line, word by word, trying to squeeze it into the allotted time.

When I get to Beyond Baroque, a lot of people are there to read and I sign up for the tenth spot of about fifty people. The place is packed. This is going to be a big show: Justin's there with Lana, yet another addition to his parade of women.

The show finally starts, and after nine readers, it's finally my turn. I know people have been going over the alloted time but thankfully, Jack has kept the water pistols holstered. I thank Sarah, the previous reader, and then I start in.

"Adam Nimoy. 'All I Want Is the Truth.' "

"She had beautiful long black hair and freckles. And a killer smile. And then, she dumped me.

"I just love it when a girl invites you to her house on the second date, jumps you on her couch and starts making out with you, then invites you back night after night for more of the same. And a week or so later, she's leading you into her bedroom and night after night it's white sheets and votive candles and lace curtains. And you start to think to yourself, 'Wow, this could really go long-term.' Then, out of nowhere, she's canceling on you at the last minute for the most ridiculous reasons. And instead of 'I'd really like to see you tonight' she's now saying: 'You can come over if you want.' And when you call her on it, she promises to make time for you, but in your gut, you know something is horribly wrong, you know that what she really means is, 'This isn't working out and it's over.' And when you confront her, she finally gives you a glib excuse like, 'Your life is so unsettled right now.' And you know that's total bullshit, you know what she really means is that you said or did something that turned her off, or the sex wasn't as good for her as you thought, or she met someone new, or she simply isn't ready for a serious relationship right now. In the acting profession, they call that 'subtext,' where a person says one thing but really means something entirely different, usually the exact opposite. In recovery, we call it 'lying.' And this girl is a terrible liar. And I should know because I'm a terrific liar. Because most alcoholics and addicts are terrific liars, so terrific that we start to believe our own bullshit.

"But I need to let go of that girl because in the end, it's over. She gave me some of the most incredible memories of my life, and for that, I love her. I would even go so far as to say I love all the women I've had the pleasure to know, including the ones who dumped me. And I'm pretty sure that's not a lie.

"And I try not to lie to them. I try not to lie. Like when I want to break up with a girl, I focus on a reason that's big enough to justify the breakup. I don't tell her about the petty stuff that's bothering me because I really don't want to hurt her feelings. I'll tell her something that puts the blame squarely on me. I'll tell her something that is totally valid and I sincerely believe. I'll say something like, 'I'm just not sure I'm ready for this relationship because . . . *my life is so unsettled right now*.'"

THE BEST APOLOGY

JUSTIN'S BEEN PISSING me off lately. We make plans for dinner or to go to a meeting together and he doesn't show or forgets or doesn't call or whatever. Now I'm just annoyed. So I finally call him on it. I usually don't call people on stuff, not now anyway. Now I just let it go and try to move on. Because when most people are called on their stuff, they just deny it or rationalize it or change the subject or counterattack about something you did to them, like, ten years ago. When that happened in the past, I would just give up and harbor my resentment and go smoke a fatty to make it all go away. But there are no fatties in AA. So anyway, with Justin, I ignore the usual rule and I call him up and tell him he's been flaking on me quite a bit and it hasn't been that much fun. He says he's sorry, which makes me feel better. The next day I get this e-mail:

Dude:

Have you ever noticed Helena [his psycho ex-girlfriend] resembles a Klingon? I'm no Trekkie. I think Trekkies are lame. I mean, I'm glad they've got a place to go and a thing to do like when drunks go to AA. And *Star Trek*—I've never been a *Star Trek* fan. The only time I got any use out of *Star Trek* was when I was a junkie in the early nineties and all we got was local programming and they'd show it at eleven pm on channel 6 and you'd sit there and escape for an hour. Other than that, fuck *Star Trek*. And then compounded by the ups and downs you've been through with your pops, every time I see anything related to the *Enterprise* or Ohura or Sulu or Kirk or you-know-who, I think to myself, "Fucking Phonies."

Fabian, in his infinite Austrian observational wisdom, has had the opportunity to perform as waitperson for both Shatner and Nimoy at the legendary Tiber restaurant in Hollywood. Of the two, Fabian comments, "They're both a pain in the ass, but you can tell Shatner is an idiot. At least Nimoy, you can tell he's smart."

Now with all my bashing of *Star Trek* and attempting to prove to you that I could care less whose Hollywood Star's kid you are, I'll tell you the following semi-funny story:

Fabian, as you know, got cable last month to watch World Cup soccer, so I've been lazing around in my off time, channel surfing. Last Friday afternoon, I happened to settle down for a Taco Bell food coma con cable and caught, from almost the beginning, *Star Trek 10* (or whatever) *The Frantic Search for Spock* and I thought to myself, "Christ, this fucking show haunts me." (I once told Helena she looked like Spock because of her eyebrows. She wasn't too happy.) So I decided to sit through *The Frantic Search* even if your dad's prosthetic eyebrows were to remind me of my crazy ex-bitch.

And what do you know? There's that scene where McCoy is channeling Spock in Spock's quarters and saying, "Why did you leave me on Genesis? Jim, why did you leave me on Genesis? I am and will be your (special) friend."

And for some reason, Adam, I swear to Allah, as corny as it is, I know, I thought to myself, "Adam loves me that much and I've left him on Genesis!"

Skip forward a couple of scenes where Kirk and the Crew are having dinner and Spock's old man comes in and berates Jim for leaving Spock, his essence, everything he was, on Genesis.

And at that moment, it all became clear to me. I thought to myself, I've never had a friend like Adam before—he would take a bullet for me, he's been sent from God to be my Guardian because he's more powerful than me, just like Spock always protects James Tiberius Kirk's dumb ass—and Spock never asks any questions—he just puts up with Kirk's lame, human shit because Spock (not your dad) is like this Buddha who has compassion for Kirk and helps him no matter what and then Kirk, in the end, is failed by his human intellect and ignorance and leaves Spock on Genesis and still Spock forgives him later.

Dude, I swear, I was watching this lame fucking movie and trying not to enjoy it because I've made it my mission to not enjoy any *Trek* bullshit on your behalf or praise Spock's work on your behalf because I know you've been hearing that shit all your life and because I love you. But there I was watching it and having this lame spiritual experience thinking, THAT'S ADAM AND ME. I'M THE LAME HUMAN.

And I turned the TV off with resolve, and this is no BS, to make my mission to be a best and most loving friend I can be to you for the rest of my life and tell you I'm sorry for being like Kirk.

You've been a godsend to me, Adam. Through all the lame chicks and my roommates and my bosses and the lame gigs—you've been the one solid, nurturing, caring thing, offering me your love, your friendship, the friendship of your children and your family, food, kindness (once, your dad's ears), patience, a generous ear, a charitable pocketbook, etc.

You're like my Spock, bro, and I didn't mean to Kirk out and leave you on Genesis. I love you. I'm sorry.

I won't leave you again.

Now let's get some crack and hookers.

xo

J.

M.O.D.

I'M IN MY directing class. By now, I seem to have totally fooled them into believing I know what the hell I'm talking about. They've been shooting and editing short films that we're screening in class. We look at each film from beginning to end. Then I praise it—there's always something to praise, even in the worst film. After that, I focus in on the problems. Jeff made a short film about a guy addicted to drugs and his girlfriend wants him to kick. It's a really good film and I tell him so. Then I focus on the beginning of the film, when the guy wakes up in the morning, goes to the closet, goes through a jacket, pulls something out, sticks it in his mouth. Not yet knowing what the film is about at this point, I don't have a clue what this guy is doing at the closet. Jeff explains.

"He's reaching into a coat pocket, takes out a vial of pills, and swallows one."

"Yeah, but I didn't know he was taking out pills. I thought he was pulling out and eating a piece of candy that he left in his jacket. I do that all the time. I mean, you know, I'll be putting on a jacket I haven't worn in a while, like, maybe all year, and I'll reach in the pocket and there will be the second half of a Baby Ruth candy bar and I'll eat it no matter what. I mean, where is the close-up here? You've only got the wide shot and we're so far away from him, he could be doing anything. Then again, I know I can be pretty slow when it comes to figuring out what's going on, but I got news for you, there are stupider people than me and they're not going to have a clue either. Why didn't you shoot the close-up?"

"That was the last thing we shot that day and we ran out of film."

"But you shot the wide of him going to the closet. This is important, folks, because when in doubt, shoot the close-up. You don't even need the wide at this point, but you do need the close-up. But even more important, where's the M.O.D.?"

"What do you mean?"

"What do you mean, what do I mean? What's an M.O.D.? Anybody."

Soren, the Swede, speaks up.

"Microphone off the dolly?"

"Oh, my God. You guys are killing me. M.O.D.! We've talked about this, like, three or four times already. When a character is put into a situation and he has to what?"

Lee raises her hand. She's from China. I call her "Silent Bob" because, though a very good filmmaker, she rarely speaks.

"He has to make a decision?"

"HE HAS TO MAKE A DECISION! Remember, 'Moment Of Decision.' That is a critical moment in your movie and you want to make the most out of it, because it adds tension and suspense to your movie and keeps the audience wondering, what's he gonna do, what's he gonna do? M.O.D.'s are much more powerful than dialogue because talk is cheap, but what people do, especially under pressure, is infinitely more revealing about their character than what they say. What is this guy's dilemma making this an M.O.D.?"

Jeff again.

"He needs to decide whether or not he's going to take the pill."

"Exactly. And good actors want to make a meal out of moments like that because a good actor knows that this is what's going through his mind: 'Should I take it or not? Maybe just one, no one will know, I've been real good, been sober for six weeks, what's one gonna hurt? I don't have to tell my sponsor, I can hide it from my girlfriend, I can function at work, I'll just take one and dump the rest, fuck it, why not.'

"You need to hold us in suspense where he pulls out the pills and looks at them and looks to see if his girlfriend is coming and reads the label and is thinking about it and is torn. Assuming you do have the time and you shoot the master, or the wide shot, which you have, and then shoot some close-ups, you can shorten how much time it takes for him to decide to take the pill. But if you don't make him wait and think about it, guess what?"

Jeff: "You can't make it longer."

"You are screwed because you cannot make it longer. And we want it longer, the audience wants it longer, we love it when we're sitting on the edge of our seats wondering what this poor schlemiel is going to do. And all you need is a close-up on that vial and the words Vicodin or Percodan or OxyContin or just the directions 'Take as needed for pain' and most people will know what's going on here.

"And if you're there and shooting this properly with a wide and a tight shot, it doesn't take that much longer to get the M.O.D. Once you're lit for the wide, it shouldn't take that long to jump in and get the tight shot of what?"

"Of him looking at the bottle, deciding."

"Right, so we have a close-up on the vial and on the guy

deciding. What else? What else might he be looking at before he makes the decision to take the pill? What else is in consideration here? Something we haven't seen that shows up in the next scene."

"The girl."

"The girl. His girlfriend, the one we find out later is trying to get him to clean up. So we might want to see his point of view of her through the door to the hallway and into the kitchen, maybe going about her business making breakfast.

"Actors love this stuff because it really gives them a chance to work through the internal conflict. It's your job as a director to find these moments in the script and serve them up to the actor, who will be very happy with you for giving him or her something to play that has some emotional impact.

"Here's another example. You tell me where the M.O.D. is and how we're going to shoot it. I'm back home for the summer after my first year at college. My parents are out of town. It's Saturday night and I'm driving around in my dad's maroon Mercedes. I got Brian riding shotgun and we drive through Westwood to pick up Glen and Rick. In twenty years, Rick will be dead from complications due to cocaine but we didn't know that then. So Rick and Glen get in and Rick has a six-pack in tow."

Here I pause and wait to see if any of the students go for the bait. Jeff gets it.

"Possible M.O.D. here."

"Why?"

"Because he's bringing a six-pack into the car."

"Exactly. But here's where the details are important because Rick shows me that none of the cans are open and the six-pack is in a brown paper bag that's folded up tight. So I don't make a big deal about it. So maybe it's a mini M.O.D.

"So Glen says there's a party up on Sunset Boulevard. We drive up there and it's on Thurston Circle, which is like this dead-end street just north of Sunset. And when we get there, the LAPD has already busted the party and there's a cop with a flashlight standing in the cul-de-sac, announcing that the party's over and waving cars to turn around and leave the neighborhood. So I make a U-turn and head back to Sunset. And when we're half a block away from Sunset, a police car makes a right onto Thurston and he's heading toward us. The street is really tight, because there are cars parked everywhere from the party, and we have to go slow. And just as the cops get to us, the driver shines a flashlight into my car, and he focuses it on the backseat. Brian and I turn around to see what the cop is looking at and there's Rick with an open beer can in his hand, right up there for the cop to see. We all yell at Rick for being a dumb shit, and when I turn back, the cop is rolling down his window and yelling at me to pull over. The cop's face is literally right next to mine, our cars are that close."

Max speaks. "M.O.D.: What are you going to do?"

"Right on, baby, M.O.D. big-time: What am I going to do? Because while that cop's yelling at me to pull over, guess what?"

"Your friends are telling you not to do it."

"They're *begging* me not to do it. 'Adam, don't do it. Don't do it, Adam. We're fucked if you do it. Don't do it. We're going to go to jail!' So what am I going to do, what am I going to do, what am I going to do? We have the audience right where we want 'em. Now, how do we really make a meal out of this thing? How do we cover it? Where do we put the camera?"

No one in the classroom moves. It's after noon, after lunch, and everyone is still a little lethargic.

Jeff is about to speak, but Cole Faran raises his hand. Cole is tall, has a deep voice, slicked-back wavy hair, a good-looking guy, and he always wears a jogging outfit. And when Cole acts in some of the films these guys produce, he's very good. Especially when he's playing a drug dealer.

"Mr. Faran, tell us how to shoot this thing."

"Well, definitely, you have to shoot the cop yelling at you."

"Yeah, right, shoot the cop. That'll get you ten to life. Okay, yeah, you put the camera on the cop. He's got a pudgy face and a butch haircut and he keeps yelling at me to pull over as he holds that flashlight and shines it in my face. What else?"

"You have to get the guys yelling at you."

"Right. I gotta get a shot of Brian next to me and Rick and Glen in the back begging me not to pull over. Maybe you do a swish pan back and forth from Brian to Rick to Glen. And they're ad-libbing all at once, saying things like, 'Adam don't do it, we're going down if you do, they'll take us to jail, blah, blah, blah.' What else?"

"There's a shot of you."

"Damn straight there's a shot of me. After all, I'm the star of this effing movie. Maybe there's an extreme close-up on my eyes or my hands gripping the steering wheel. If you have the time, you can have a freaking field day with this thing. So what do I do? What do I do? What do I do? Because I gotta tell you, and this is a note I might give to the actor; because here's what's going on in my mind at this moment in time. It just so happens that five years before, when I was fourteen, I was busted for driving my mother's car without a license. They mugshotted and fingerprinted me, but that time they let me go. Now I'm nineteen and I'm scared shitless they're going to stick me in jail. That's how I might heighten the internal conflict of what do I do, what do I do.

"But what else? What else can we do to make even more of a meal out of this thing?"

Lee raises her hand.

"Yeah, Silent Bob."

"Slow motion?"

"Exactly, you can slow the film down. You can overcrank the camera and slow-mo everything down. That'll stretch the moment out and no one will complain because you'll be giving the audience a real good ride. Close-up on me in slow-mo, then my point-of-view of the cop silently mouthing off to me in slo-mo, and then I turn to the boys, and the same thing with them."

Silent Bob speaks again. "And you can add some music."

"Bingo, like maybe some intense Hitchcock violins from *Psycho*, or you can go in the opposite direction by using, like, some cool jazzy bass line or something. You see how it works? Even though all of this happened in a matter of seconds, you can keep the tension going by cutting from me to the cop yelling to the guys in the car yelling and then back to me to see what I'm gonna do. All right, let's move on and look at the other films as we only have about twenty minutes left."

Alex jumps in. "So what the hell did you do?"

"What do you mean?"

"Did you pull over or what?"

"What difference does it make? The point is, you need to be able to get the film you need to make these moments happen because you can't just make it up in the editing room if there's nothing to cut to."

"Oh, c'mon, man. You can't leave us all hanging."

"What are you talking about, man, this class isn't about the story of my life, it's about yours."

Everyone starts to groan at this point. I've got 'em right where I want 'em.

"All right, all right. What do I do, what do I do, what do I do? I'll tell you what I do. I step on the fucking gas."

Cole: "I knew it!"

Barbara pipes up. "Did the cops catch you?"

"Did the cops catch me? What do you think? Maybe we should take a vote."

Soren the Swede speaks. "Just tell us."

"All right, whatever. So I step on the gas and drive the half block back to Sunset. I know I've got a jump on the cops because the street is so tight, he has to go back up to the cul-de-sac to turn around. I get to Sunset and make a left turn and floor it and my dad's Mercedes shoots out onto Sunset Boulevard like a rocket. Brian rolls down his window and throws out a joint and some Quaaludes. He turns around and yells at Rick to throw the beers out the window, which he does. Then Brian asks if anyone's carrying and Rick says he's got that bag of purple buds his brother just bought and I yell to Rick to toss it but Rick won't do it because he's afraid his brother's going to beat the shit out of him. So I'm driving like a motherfucker around these curves on Sunset and the three of us start yelling at Rick to toss the buds, but he won't do it, and Brian has to take off his seat belt and lean into the back and he and Glen beat the shit out of Rick until they finally grab the buds and Brian throws them out the window into a bed of ivy. And this whole time I never see the cops behind me, we're far enough ahead and there are enough curves and I know we still have the lead.

"And we're rounding the last bend before we get to Veteran Avenue and UCLA, but this is my neighborhood and I know exactly where we are and I know that Bentley Avenue is coming up. And at the last second I make a hard right onto Bentley and I turn off my lights and take my foot off the brake. And I look in my rearview mirror, and within seconds I see that cop car, lights flashing, race by down Sunset Boulevard, passing Bentley without even seeing us.

"And the guys in my car are all happy and celebrating and shit. They're high-fiving and laughing and patting me on the back. And the last cut of this sequence? The very last shot we see in this episode? A tight close-up on me because I'm the only one who's not happy about this situation, I'm the only one who knows this is totally fucked up, I'm the one who's finally starting to realize that maybe I'm running with the wrong crowd."

TYPICAL CONVERSATION WITH A TEENAGE DAUGHTER #312: LET'S GO TO THERAPY

IT'S WINTER AND night. I have to pick up Maddy and take her to therapy. I'm driving to the design studio where she has a part-time job and I call her to say I'm two minutes away. A minute and a half later she calls me and I know she's outside and I'm not there yet and she's just going to have to wait. Because I just spoke to her, I ignore the call. Then I get another call from her and I ignore that one too—and there she is out front.

"Dad, why don't you answer your phone?!"

"Because I just spoke to you, and if I'm thirty seconds late, I start getting calls from you, which is ridiculous."

This quiets her down.

"Mom tells me you might want to go in to talk to Shayna by yourself."

"Dad, I'm not going in by myself, you're coming in with me."

"I don't know. I think you may have some things you might want to talk to her about alone."

"Dad, I hate it when you do this to me. You either go in with me or I'm not going at all because I have nothing to say to her."

At this point I don't say a thing because it's just a waste of energy and Maddy's too headstrong and I never end up changing her mind anyway. So I just let it go. She always says she doesn't want to go to therapy, and then when we come out, she always high-fives me because we manage to get through so much stuff together.

As we pass the streetlights, I can see her long brown hair and her white T-shirt under a deep blue V-neck sweater. She's wearing the necklace I bought her at Tiffany's for her fourteenth birthday. She's always wearing that necklace. It's a silver heart on a long thick silver chain that nearly reaches to her waist.

I gently squeeze her little pointed nose hoping she'll lighten up.

"What should we talk about in therapy?"

"I don't know, Dad. Right now we don't have any major issues and I have so much homework."

I pull up to Shayna's office, and coming out of the building is a man and a teenage girl who is clearly his daughter. She's walking ahead of him and they're not talking, they don't look too happy.

Maddy watches them get in their car and drive away.

"Dad, those guys were just like us."

"Yeah, except they weren't happy like we are when we come out of therapy."

"Dad, what do you think of my sandals?" They're the ones with silver straps.

"Oh, I love them. They're so pretty."

Then I notice she's wearing her cutoff jean shorts, the ones that go way up high, and she's not wearing tights and it's her skinny white legs and bare feet in sandals and it's the middle of winter.

"Maddy, aren't you cold in those clothes?"

"No, Dad."

"Maddy, I really don't think those shorts are appropriate in this weather."

"Dad, don't criticize me, I am not in the mood right now," and she storms off.

We settle down in Shayna's office.

"Your dad left me a message saying you might want to talk to me alone."

Maddy just smiles so I feel compelled to chime in.

"She said she wouldn't come in at all if I didn't come in with her."

"Well, I'll keep an eye on the time and maybe the last fifteen minutes we'll kick your dad out and you and I will have some time alone."

Maddy just smiles and Shayna realizes something's up.

"In fact, why don't we kick your dad out now for fifteen minutes and we can go out and get him in the waiting room."

I immediately get up and leave.

I walk back to the waiting room, but the light sucks and some psychotic patient has taken a pair of scissors and literally cut a recent issue of *The New Yorker* to pieces. So I decide to go to my car and get my book. On my way out, I peek through the blinds to see Maddy because Shayna's office has floor-to-ceiling windows and there's a walkway around the office, so you can look in through the Levelors. I can just make out Maddy and her high shorts and skinny legs and silver sandals. I can see her mouth moving and she's talking a mile a minute. I'm so glad she has the opportunity to get things off her chest. I'm thinking and actually saying to myself right out there on the walkway, "I love that girl." Sometimes I like to pretend that if I were seeing her for the first time, if I came home from a long, difficult journey and someone pointed her out to me and said she was my daughter, I'd feel so lucky to know that she was mine.

I get my book and head back to the waiting room where I turn on the overhead light and read. And read. And read. Forty-five minutes later, at the end of the session, they finally come out all smiling and Maddy says, "Dad, you have to pay Shayna."

And I'm like, "I'm glad you managed to think of something to talk about."

We get back into the car.

"So what did you talk about?"

"Oh, stuff like boys and friends and drugs and school."

"What kind of drugs?"

"Coke and crystal meth."

"Are you or anyone you know doing that stuff?"

"No, not really. I'm just curious about it."

"You didn't talk to Shayna about pot?"

"What about it?"

"How many times have you done it?"

"Oh, I don't know."

Then we drive up Barrington Avenue past University High, past the gate that I came out of during lunch one spring day in 1974 to move my car, past the spot where the cops stopped me and told me to breathe on them. I tell this to Maddy.

"Why did they tell you to do that, Dad?"

"Because I was a long-hair and they wanted to know if I had pot breath. Then I breathed my pot-free breath on them and they let me go."

"Did you ever get high at school?"

"Maddy, believe it or not, I was never, ever high a single day in school during my entire three years at Uni."

"That's smart."

"I'm glad you think so, honey. But when I got home, I lit up."

"Where were Noni and Poppi?"

"Poppi was working."

"Where was Noni?"

"She didn't seem to care as long as I didn't do it in the house."

"So, then, you shouldn't care about me doing it."

"How much are you doing it?"

Maddy just gives me one of her little sarcastic smiles and turns away. We drive past the intersection of Wilshire and Federal, where, back in June '74, I managed to get into a head-on collision with an eighty-year-old man who could barely see. No one got hurt, but the guy sitting shotgun was even older and was wearing these dark blinders over his eyes and he stumbled out of the car with a white cane, yelling at me, "I saw the whole damn thing and it was your fault!" I wasn't much older than Maddy and I'm pretty sure I was stoned at the time. I was driving the '68 Buick Riviera. Dad was getting rid of it because he now had the maroon Mercedes.

"Answer me, Maddy, how much are you doing it?

"Sometimes. Occasionally. It's like Shayna told you, Dad, everyone's doing it. Everyone."

"Who, Jenna? I know Laura and Alison do it because I busted them at Mom's art opening."

"Dad, they weren't doing it."

"Yeah, right. Whatever. Talk about pot breath. I just want you to be careful."

"You can't say I can't do it if you did it."

"I'm not saying you can't do it. I'm saying be careful or you'll wake up thirty years later reaching for the bong in the morning like me, and then it's off to AA. Because addiction runs in our family and, like Shayna said, it could easily happen to you. I can't tell you how many girls I've heard speak at meetings who became alcoholics and addicts before they were even old enough to take a legal drink."

"What do you mean?"

"I mean these young girls get up and talk about how they ended up strung out on Hollywood Boulevard and all they wanted to do was stick a needle in their arm and get high and they're so happy that they got into the program and they've been sober for three years and these girls are only like nineteen or twenty years old. When you come to a meeting with me, you'll see."

Maddy just sits there and takes it in. I'm hoping I'm having an effect on her. If I can just keep my kids out of rehab. She sits there, thinking. She's smart. She's a very good student and I know she's thinking about this.

And then she turns to me with her pretty little face.

"Dad, will you buy me a pipe?"

———

I'm in the car with Jonah taking him to school. He's been going to Garrett's to work with him and Jason on a video presentation they have on the first ten amendments to the Constitution, and they're going over their project before school starts.

"How is it working with Garrett and Jason?"

"It's good. I mean, they're kind of nerdy but they get good grades."

"And you get along with those guys?"

"I get along with everyone."

He says this in an offhand way, like he doesn't want to brag but he's very proud of the fact that he can make friends easily and I'm very proud of this quality in him. Now, if he can just get good grades like the nerds. He's got a little plastic gorilla in his hands, and the gorilla is holding a machine gun.

"So what's with the gorilla and the other toy soldiers and stuff?"

"We're using these to show the ten amendments. Like we have Batman slide down a rope into gorilla's house and gorilla comes out and says, 'Get out of my house.' [He makes a machine gun noise.] Then after he shoots Batman, he says, 'Right to bear arms, motherfucker!!'"

"That's what you're putting in your video?"

"Except for the *motherfucker* . . ."

———

When we get to school, I pull over and he gets out of the car.

"Do you have your lunch?"

"Got it right here."

"Do you need any money?"

"No, I'm all right."

"Good luck on your project. I loves you."

"Thanks, Dad. Loves you too."

And I kiss him good-bye. When he walks into the schoolyard, he looks back at me and waves. I sit in my car, waving and watching him. He walks on farther and then turns around and we wave to each other again. I still don't go.

And just before he's out of sight, he turns back again to find me still sitting there, and he smiles and waves one last time and then he's gone.

THE SOMEBODY GIRL

I'M ON THE East Coast, helping to chaperone Jonah's eighth-grade class on their social studies field trip, and I'm unpacking at the hotel wondering what shoes to wear on the streets of Philadelphia tomorrow. It depends on whether it's going to rain again—more like pour. My roommate, Steve, seems like a very clever guy and he has a pretty girlfriend. They're also chaperones on this trip. There are ten of us and we're taking eighty eighth-graders to Philadelphia and Gettysburg and Washington. I thought they'd be sharing a room, Steve and his girlfriend, but I guess not.

Our hotel is out in the middle of nowhere. The view out the window is to the atrium, where there's a wedding party in full swing. It's nine o'clock and the hotel assures us it'll go only until ten. Loud music and it's right next to our room. We open our ground-floor window and there's a table of guests sitting right there, looking at us looking at them.

Beautiful city, Philadelphia, pouring rain.

"Excuse me," I say to our tour guide, who's perfectly dressed in Colonial attire, including a ponytail. "I think the kids need to take a minute to get their rain gear off the bus because we weren't ready for this. Otherwise, they're going to be miserable."

He agrees, and we open the bus and the kids get what they need, but we still end up getting soaked.

I need to find a pen. The one I'm using now to write in my journal isn't working very well. I need to find a good pen. I need to find out where I am because I know we're somewhere outside of Philadelphia. Otherwise, I feel like I'm lost. Or better yet, I need to find out *who I am* because there are some people out there who think I'm a nobody, or, at the very least, that I'm not a Somebody like them. And sometimes, I still wake up in the morning in a panic worrying that I'm *not* a Somebody and that I'll never be a Somebody. And if I don't immediately get up and jog it off, I know the panic will totally consume me. In my recovery, I'm trying very hard to keep things simple, One Day at a Time, as they say. I need to find a good pen.

"Is your father Leonard Nimoy?" Steve asks as we unpack and get ready for bed. Steve's not a bad-looking guy now that I take a closer look, although he was a little cold when we first met at LAX. He's got a bit of a cool look with the black T-shirt and jeans and black-framed glasses. And when he said he thought marriage was overrated, well, he kind of had me there. But when he said he could have a looker in his bed almost any night of the week, well, he kind of lost me there. Even if it's true.

It's just a cheap hotel room, but it's clean and it'll do. There's a crack in the bathroom sink and the bedspreads are gold-colored and stiff.

"Christina said you're Leonard Nimoy's son."

"That's what they tell me."

It's one of my clever little stock replies. After forty years of being asked that question, I've learned to have these ready. "We're just good friends, actually" is another one I like to use. It's a line I stole from Paul McCartney in *A Hard Day's Night*. "He's very clean" is another one of my favorite lines from that movie.

"I was at his photography exhibit opening at Antoine's restaurant," Steve goes on to say as he's putting his T-shirts and
boxers into one of the dresser drawers. "The nude women exhibit."

"Oh, yeah, the nude women," I echo.

There's a woman at that opening at Antoine's restaurant and
she's looking at me. She's checking me out and she doesn't
mind that I see her doing it so I check her out right back. And
she's pretty, very pretty: the kind of brunette I'd like to be with,
the type I could be happy with. The type that I could learn to
love, the type I could spend the rest of my life with. As long
as she's not psycho—or dumb. But I know she's not. Dumb.
Because I know who she is: She's a Somebody, a Somebody
Girl. And she's not too young. In fact, best of all, she has some
of the lines of age. But then again, she's a Somebody and I'm
a nobody, or at least some Somebodies I know seem to think
I'm a nobody. And sometimes, I find myself believing them.
Steve's a nobody too; otherwise I would have recognized him
because there are several Somebodies here.

Steve pulls back the hotel curtains and the wedding partiers
are still sitting at their table looking bored, which is probably
why they're looking at us looking at them. It's a shitty hotel
really, the kind that would sell off the atrium to a wedding
party while the other guests pull back their curtains to watch.
But what kind of hotel do you expect for eighty eighth-graders
and ten chaperones?

But she's really just perfect, the Somebody Girl. Pretty but
not too pretty, just right really. Beautiful eyes, white jeans,
designer sandals. Her husband's a Somebody too. Maybe they
swing. Maybe it's an open marriage. Or maybe she's bored. It's
crowded here at Antoine's, once the place to be, or so Steve

tells me, because he knows Antoine and the restaurant used to be the place to go for food and drinks and cocaine.

I've got to get out of here. The Somebody Girl and her Somebody Husband, the nude women hanging on the walls, the room full of Somebodies. The Somebody hosts who are mad at me about something and look at me like I'm a nobody, like they don't even know who I am or what I'm doing here. I have got to get the hell out of here.

"Yeah, I was at your dad's photography opening," Steve says, looking up at me, now that he's finished unpacking. "The nude women."

"Yeah," I reply, "the nude women."

HOLY HOLLY

SHE KEEPS WINKING at me at the meetings. She catches my eye from across the room and gives me a look that says, "Come on, baby. It's going to be good, really good. I promise."

Sometimes I just get lonely, so incredibly lonely. And you can't hold a cyber girl, you can't hold them and caress them and breathe them in.

So I finally say, "Okay, let's go."

But then Holly has a day or two of seller's/buyer's remorse and is afraid of the intensity of her feelings and gets nervous and wants to back out. And when I give her the space to do it, she quickly recants and invites me over to "hang out."

And it *was* really good, just like she promised. That first night, we wrecked her place. Now I'm over there all the time because I want more—just like an addict.

Justin comes over to me during the break at the Monday night meeting. "Dude, Holly told me you're a tiger in the bedroom."

"What the fuck? That's bullshit."

"I swear to you. She said you guys have been totally pushing the envelope."

"Oh, my God. I gotta put the kibosh on all that. She's the one pushing the envelope. I'm just trying to keep up. That girl's ten years younger than me and she's wearing me out."

And then, a few weeks later, we're in her apartment, heating it up on her olive velour couch. I stand up to take a breather and she follows me. Her cat sits nearby. Holly is bathed in the late afternoon light. Gorgeous body. Soft, white skin. I hold her close and we sway to the music.

"I know that if I ever relapse I would lose you."

This comes out of nowhere.

"Yes, you would."

I echo the sentiment because deep down I know this is never going to last. The physical connection seems so good but I've been noticing other issues cropping up that tell me that maybe we're not meant to be together after all. I'm now seeing the many differences between us and maybe, someday soon, this thing is going to crash and burn. Only now, she's given me an out, though I hope to God, for her sake, that she *doesn't* relapse.

Two weeks go by. As usual, I'm over at her place wanting more: candles and music and her couch and me hovering over her. And just as it starts to get hot, she starts in.

"There's something I think you should know."

"What do I need to know at this exact moment? Wait a minute, let me guess. You're gay."

"No."

"You're bi, which I am totally okay with."

"No."

"You're seeing somebody else."

"No."

"You want to see somebody else."

"No, Adam."

I'm looking in her eyes, those incredible eyes that need to tell me something, something I've known since this conversation began. I just didn't want to say it.

"You went out."

"I went out."

"When?"

"Two weeks ago. The night of the Rose Bowl. I was with my girlfriends and we went to a bar to drink and, oh, Adam, I know it was so stupid to go but what was I supposed to do? I thought I could handle it, but everyone was having so much fun and it looked so good and I know I should have just gone home but I didn't."

"So you drank."

"And did some coke—like all night. I was a wreck the next day."

I'm up and off of her now, sitting on the couch, staring at the candle. Her legs start to close . . . along with our relationship.

"Don't be mad at me, Adam. Don't pout, it doesn't suit you."

I'm a professional pouter, been doing it most of my life. Note to myself: Need to keep working on not pouting.

It was during this conversation that she fessed up to the fact that she also went out at Lawrence's party. Lawrence the lawyer with the beach house and the teenage bedroom with the shag carpet and the stuffed animals that belonged to a total stranger. All that blow in the bathroom—I could smell it.

And that was my out.

Maybe she relapsed to push me away. Maybe she set me up with the "If I ever relapse I would lose you" line just to get rid of me. Maybe I should have seen it coming.

I do enjoy Holly's laughter and her smarts, and there is rarely a dull moment after she turns off the lights and breaks out the candles. But now I don't think I'm helping her with her recovery and I'm pretty sure she's not helping me with mine.

And so I walked.

And she let me go.

KID MONK BARONI

WE'VE BEEN HAVING this meeting at Chris Kelton's house. Chris and his neighbor Michael and me. We meet on Thursday nights in the backyard. It's really nice, and on some nights we have as many as ten people. I'm the secretary. The format is like other book-study meetings: We read a chapter from the Big Book and then go around the circle sharing based on what we've read or anything else that comes to mind.

"Hi, I'm Adam and I'm an alcoholic and addict. I liked the part of the reading about how resentments are the number one reason for drinking and relapses, because I've had so much resentment in my life, the source of much of it being my relationship with my dad, although as I do the work in the program, I'm becoming less and less sure of how much I need to hold him responsible.

"There was a screening of a movie he made in 1952 called *Kid Monk Baroni,* a B movie that my dad starred in when he was only twenty-one. The screening was at the Egyptian Theater in Hollywood and, oh, I don't know, I didn't want to go, I just don't like to go to those things. But I didn't want him to think I was punishing him for some reason by not going, and I didn't want my mind to have to obsess and work overtime to justify not going because that takes so much time and effort, and I *was* curious to see the movie because I hadn't seen it in twenty-five or thirty years, so I said I'd do it.

"And I almost never go out in public with my dad anymore and when I got there, it was just like it always was: He was the sun drawing all these people to his glow as they came for autographs and pictures and handshakes and smiles and on and on. People gathering all around him. And there I was standing in the shadows, watching this from the outside, out in the dark. And it made me think about my own life and how I never thought it would come to this, how I thought I would have my own glow and find my own success whether it was practicing law or directing shows or maybe even movies. But for a whole bunch of reasons, not the least of which were the drinking and using, things didn't quite go the way I expected.

"And it was so incredibly painful, for a minute, it all came back to me being on the outside, watching this going on, because that was the issue of my life, not having a close relationship with him and then having to cope with the weirdness, the constant adulation and idol worship. And I think that's partly why my drinking and using went on for so long: to kill the pain of comparing my world to his, of not measuring up somehow, of him so incredibly focused on his career and so phenomenally successful at it. Because for me, that's the hardest part of growing up the son of a celebrity: While you're a kid, you kind of bask in the glow, simply because you're surrounded by it. But when you're old enough to move out and go off to college and be on your own, things get pretty cold real fast. And there's an occasional solar flare and some of that sunshine is directed your way when someone asks, 'Are you related?'

"But pretty soon, you figure out it has nothing to do with you. It's *their* career not yours, it's *their* success not yours, and it can get very frustrating in terms of why you can't also generate that kind of heat and get that kind of attention on your own. I mean, even if you work hard and even if you're confident of your abilities, it gets very confusing and disillusioning as to why you haven't been able to make it work for you the way they made their talent and hard work work for them. And you start to believe that there's something missing from your life, that you've got this gaping hole and the only way to fill it and feel better about yourself is to drink or use because there's instant gratification with all that and then, while you're high, you can fantasize how important you're going to be someday and that you'll show everyone, *you'll show your celebrity father that he's not the only one in the family who can generate that kind of heat*. I don't know, I mean, I know that a lot of this is all superficial anyway, the fame and the adulation but knowing that doesn't always take away the pain of your perceived shortcomings and your lack of success.

"But with the work I do in the program, I just feel so much less anxious and more content than I did before I got here. And more often than not, I can now let go of all that frustration and live in my own skin and be content with the fact that I have accomplished a hell of a lot in my own life. And that doesn't mean that I've become complacent and that I've given up on my hopes and dreams. And sometimes, the intense craving for more success comes back to me. When I see him out there in the crowd, the craving comes back and there's still a little bit of panic that my life is slipping away and that I'll never get to where I want to be, that I'll never generate any real heat of my own.

"And, I don't know, I just, I think that's plenty for tonight.

"Thanks for letting me share."

HOLD FOR JONAH

I PICK JONAH up from school.

"Dad, can we go to the bank today?"

"Not today, honey, because they close in twenty minutes and we'll never get there in time. Maybe tomorrow because you know you owe me some money for that iPod."

"Why don't we switch banks, Dad? Yours is never open."

"I like it because there's never a line there."

"But it's never open."

"That makes it harder for you to take out all your money. You would have emptied your account by now if the bank were open all the time."

And then we go back to my place so that he can do his homework. I'm living in a nice apartment in Santa Monica now. Maddy helped pick it out and she helped me to set it up. But she still won't stay over. At least it's nice to have Jonah there.

He works for about an hour and says he's done, which I don't quite believe, but we look at his grades online and they're pretty darn good, which is terrific in light of how much he struggled last year. Then he picks up my Fender Strat and starts wailing on "Hangar 18," making it impossible for me to concentrate. I tell him to use the headphones but he refuses. Note for note he's perfect on "Hangar 18"—his fingers are long and elegant now, and it's like poetry watching him play. And I like Dave Mustaine and Megadeth as much as the next guy but

I've heard this song about fifty times over the past two weeks and it's starting to wear. Sometimes, I wonder where I went wrong—our musical tastes used to be so similar and now he's gone straight to metal. It's like I put in an order for a Deadhead and got a Metalhead instead. I beg him to do something else just for another hour and he says fine, that he wants to ride his skateboard down to the surf shop to look at surfboards and stuff, and I say okay, I'll come get him in an hour.

After he leaves, I check my e-mail and find one from Richard the Tall, the agent I've by now recently met for lunch. He says he's read my material, but instead of commenting on it directly he suggests I write a novel about a girl like Holly and a guy like me who aren't meant to be together but have sex and eventually love each other in their own way. "They should take a trip, like the road trip in *Sideways*, that forces them closer together than they're ready for, while they reveal their personal stories and are tested by what comes their way." I reply back thanking him for taking the time and telling him that I'm going to brainstorm ideas for the road trip novel.

I have no intention of ever contacting him again.

The phone rings and it's Jonah. He wants me to come down to check out the new surfboard he's going to buy for six hundred dollars.

"You're not buying a new board."

"Oh, my God, Dad, you said that if I get good grades I could get a new board."

"I said by the end of the semester, if you have good grades, we would look into getting you one for Hanukkah."

"Are you joking?!"

I love that line: "Are you joking?" Maddy and Jonah both use it when they refuse to believe something I've just said.

"Are you joking?! Dad, that is *not* what you said."

"Jonah, that is *exactly* what I said and you have the worst habit of changing the deal to get what you want right now. Next time, get it in writing and we won't have to go through this."

"Oh, my God, Dad, you said tomorrow we could go to the bank because I'm paying for this with my own money."

"I said we could go to the bank to get the money you already owe me for the iPod."

"Come on, Dad, I had them put the board on hold for me and everything."

"Jonah, you are not getting a board and I'm coming down there right now."

And then he switches gears and his mood changes into Mr. Happy-Go-Lucky.

"Okay, Dad, see you later."

Click.

He always says that "see you later" whether I'm going to see him in five minutes or the next day. I just love that. And I love the way he can change his tone on a dime: He'll switch from totally argumentative to complete and willing capitulation. Actually, what I think is going on here is that he felt some pressure from the salespeople and he now feels obliged to buy the stuff and he wants me to come down and play bad cop to get him off the hook. We've been through this scenario before.

So I drive down there and the second I walk in the door Jonah comes up to me.

"Dad, please, please, can I get it? I'll use my own money. Please. Please, Dad."

Standing behind him are two salespeople, a guy and a girl, just standing there waiting. I know this is just part of the show to prove to them that he really wants the board even though he knows he can't have it.

It's late in the day, almost nightfall, and there's not much traffic in the store right now and so the salespeople have nothing better to do than to stand around and put the thumbscrews on Jonah and then on me. The guy's name is Tim and he's always trying to sell me something, and the girl, a blonde, is wearing a short skirt that shows off her incredible legs. I took my first surf lesson from Tim about a year ago, and now, when I see him in the water and ask him questions about surfing, he's always short with me, like, "Hey, pal, we're not on the clock here so don't try to hit me up for some freebies."

Laid out at Tim's feet on the showroom floor is a beautiful epoxy surfboard. It's white with red trim. There's a strip of masking tape on it that reads, "Hold for Jonah." Next to it is a silver board bag that you use for carrying the surfboard around. It also has a strip of masking tape that reads, "Hold for Jonah." And next to the board bag is a stomp pad and a leash—and I'm not even going to try to explain what those are for but they both have masking tape that reads, "Hold for Jonah." It's all part of the territory of raising a fourteen-year-old boy who just loves rock 'n' roll and surfing and back-to-back episodes of *The Dave Chapelle Show* and *Family Guy* and who just loves to buy things.

"Dad, please, please, let me get it. I told them I would pick everything up tomorrow, after we go to the bank."

I just look up at Tim and smile.

"Hey, Tim."

Tim says hey and smiles back, because he knows what's going on. The blonde runs off with her incredible legs to answer the phone. I'm still smiling when I turn to Jonah.

"I hear Hanukkah is early this year."

"Dad, please."

"It's really a pretty board, but you're not getting it. Tim, will you excuse us while we go off to have a little powwow."

Tim's still smiling. "I totally understand."

I gently lead Jonah to the back of the store.

"Dad, why won't you let me? You said we could go to the bank tomorrow."

"I said we could go to get the money you owe me for the iPod."

"I've wanted that board for, like, months."

"Well, you're going to have to wait a little longer."

"Why won't you let me?"

Now I put my hands on Jonah's cheeks and squeeze them together. Jonah's got short hair now and he's tall and in high school, but he's still a boy. I slip into my Elmer Fudd imitation.

"You know, Yonah, you ah soooo wucky to have me watching out for you. 'Cause if I wasn't awound, yo bank account would be empty wight now."

"Dad, this isn't funny. I want that surfboard."

"You weewee have noooo idea what a wucky guy you are to have me awound."

"Dad, pleeeease! Why can't I get it, Dad? Why can't I?"

I start holding Jonah tight and give him little kisses because we're standing behind the T-shirt racks and no one can see us. Then I get a little distracted because they have such great stuff in the store, like the nine-foot surfboards hanging overhead with vibrant color patterns airbrushed on them. And I'm holding Jonah tight just like I used to when he was small. I remember how cute he was as a little boy and how I just wanted to squeeze him all the time. I do this with Maddy too, I hold her tight with such intensity, just like I did when she was little and had curly hair and took her dolls everywhere and I'd hug and squeeze her. And that's what I do now that she's sixteen and he's fourteen, I just remember what I was feeling when they were small, the intensity of those feelings all comes back to me and I hug them even tighter. And they still let me do it. In front of their friends they still let me hold them and kiss them and they don't care what the others think—or maybe they want them to know how much their dad still loves them, even if he did move out of the house.

"Why not, Dad? Just tell me why not."

Now I put on the tough parent act.

"Because you just got a new RAZR phone two weeks ago and last week you got the iPod and now you're on to this. You're way into getting stuff, my friend, and it's not a good thing."

"Yeah, but Michael has a new phone *and* an iPod *and* a new surfboard."

"I don't care about what Michael gets. I care about you, and you need to learn that just because you want it doesn't mean you're going to get it."

"But it's my money."

"Yes, but you're a fourteen-year-old boy, which means you're a minor, which means you need my permission to get into that bank account and *you don't have it.* In another four years you'll be eighteen and you can blow what's left of your Bar Mitzvah money on whatever you want, but by then you're going to have to figure out how to pay for your car insurance."

Jonah takes a breather. This all seems to be sinking in. I think I've gotten through to him.

"I don't do this because it's fun for me. I don't like saying no, like, twenty times and I hate fighting with you about this all the time. But you need to learn that sometimes good things come to those who wait, and when you set your mind on something, you have zero in the patience department. And did you even ask for Carlos to get him to give you a discount?"

"No. He's not here tonight."

"Well, we need to talk to him because six hundred dollars for a piece of painted foam is ridiculous and we drop so much money in this place I know he'll give us a break. But all that's going to have to wait until we get your report card and until Hanukkah arrives, which is only six weeks away."

"But they went through the trouble of pulling all this stuff out for me."

I knew it. He felt bad about making them go through all the trouble without making a sale. It's so cute the way he cares about other people's feelings . . . other people's except mine in these "why can't I have it?" situations.

"Jonah, believe me, they do this all the time. That's their job."

"Well, will you tell them?"

"No problem. I'll explain the whole situation to Tim and I promise you, he'll totally understand."

"All right. Thanks, Dad."

We walk back to the front of the store and I explain everything to Tim, and he assures Jonah that when he's ready, if they don't have that board in the shop, he can get it in two days. And Jonah bends down and starts peeling off all the masking tape on the board and the bag and the leash and the stomp pad, the tape on all that expensive new stuff that he just had to have, the tape that reads, "Hold for Jonah."

MY NEW NOT-SO-BRILLIANT CAREER:
THE EYES HAVE IT

NIGHTTIME AT A STOPLIGHT. Beautiful silky blonde in a Mercedes on my right. I wave to her. She waves back. Maybe my age. No ring. She drives off. End of that affair.

Now it's Thursday morning. My directing students drag themselves into class. They're totally lethargic and beat-up because they've been out making their little films and they're really getting the message that filmmaking is hard work. The lecture I'm supposed to give them today is "Adam Nimoy's Incredibly Wonderful Lecture on Story Structure," because I'm always emphasizing story and performance over filmmaking technique. This is the biggest problem with new filmmakers: They get so caught up in the technical aspects of filmmaking—the camera, the lighting, the editing—that they forget we're just storytellers who happen to tell our tales visually.

This is critical to what I'm trying to teach in class. But because they're so fried, they're not responding to the lecture.

"Listen, you guys, I know you've been out shooting and you're tired and guess what? *Welcome to filmmaking.* Because how you feel right about now is how I feel after prepping my show before I even start to shoot. Because, as you know, prepping things properly is a *huge* amount of work. Forget about an eight- to ten-week film shoot, I'm talking about just prepping a one-hour show that shoots for eight days. By the time you take over the set, you're already tired from the story meetings and the casting sessions and the location scouts and breaking down the script and the meetings with various departments. So when you get to the set, you have to find things to keep your energy going otherwise the crew will go right down the sinkhole with you because they've been going at it for weeks if not months of thirteen- to sixteen-hour days and they are *really* beat. One of the things I do to keep my energy up is eat all day because if I'm not constantly fueling the fire, I will just pass out. The other thing that keeps me going is working with the talent, the actors, because if you've done your job, if you've prepped the show or the picture to the best of your ability, you should be able to enjoy watching great performances all day. And that is one of the reasons I try not to watch the monitor when I'm directing. Most directors sit and watch the monitor during a take, but if the camera is not moving, if it's a static over-the-shoulder shot on an actor or a close-up, I'm standing right next to the camera. Why do you think I do that?"

"Because you're closer to them and can see them."

"Yeah, I can see them, I mean, really see them. That's why, sometimes, I just don't get the monitor. It's like sitting in house seats at a play and you're tenth row center and you're watching the whole thing from your iPod. You're trying to watch these great performances on this little screen. I mean, it makes no sense to me. It's like I'm one step removed and what's the point? And then you yell direction at, say, two people making love and you're ten yards away sitting at the monitor? 'A little more romantic maybe! How about a little more tongue in that kiss? Give her a little more tongue!' I mean, I just don't get it. And when the camera assistant measures the focal distance from the camera to the actor, where does he measure to?

When he walks that measuring tape out to the actor, where does he stop?"

"The nose?"

"The nose? I don't think so."

"The eye?"

"Yes, the eye. We focus on the eye because the eyes have the truth, the eyes are windows to the soul, and that's exactly what I'm looking at when I stand next to the camera because I'm just looking for a little truth. All I want is the truth. And I have a harder time seeing it if I'm looking at a TV monitor off the set. If the camera is moving or it's a stunt scene or there are a lot of complicated elements involved, yes, of course, you sit at the monitor. Sometimes you have two monitors with A and B cameras going at the same time, and that *really* drives me nuts. My son, Jonah, can keep his right eye steady while his left eye drifts off to look at something else. I think Homer Simpson can do it too. But I can't do it. So, as much as I can, I'm by the camera. And *you* should be thinking about standing by the camera. Because when you give a helpful note to an actor and right then and there you see a change in performance, I guarantee that's going to pump up your energy level because there's nothing like it. And when you're standing there, when you're standing next to the camera and you call 'Action,' I urge you to remind yourself that *everything you've done in your life has led you to that moment*, standing there, totally focused on the actors, *being in the moment*. It's a powerful feeling and most actors will appreciate it when you're right there with them.

"I was once working on a show and the star was one hell of a mean motherfucker. And the first day of shooting, we're doing some scenes in his apartment and I'm standing by the camera watching everything and after a few shots this actor, the star of the show, yells out, 'We have a director! Ladies and gentlemen, we have a real director on the set! We have a man who actually watches performance!' And I'm feeling, like, real good about this. Real good. And during the rest of the shoot we were out on location. And because that actor was a mean sonovabitch who looked hungover every morning of the shoot, that man kicked my ass all over this town. Because this guy had done a lot of TV and a lot of movies and he was a very good filmmaker in his own right and we had a lot of action pieces and some of it was definitely over my head. In fact, I learned a lot from watching him direct himself, shooting through smoke and fire and shit. But even when we were just shooting regular dramatic scenes this guy was now tearing into me.

"We were shooting one scene where I asked a guest star to turn more to camera and this sick dick came right up to me, right in my face like literally two inches away, and looked me dead in the eye and said, 'Are you directing my actors? Are you directing my actors?! Don't direct my actors.' And he was a good-looking guy with the most beautiful eyes. I swear he had turquoise eyes with just a dash of yellow. I stood my ground and said, 'I'm just asking her to open to camera. There's no problem here.' And I didn't blink and I didn't take a single step back. And finally this guy turns and walks back to his mark. And I turn to the camera operator who was also a tough mofo but we had become friends because he respected a lot of what I was trying to do. So I turn to the camera operator, and on the sly he winks at me and gives me the thumbs-up. That's another way to stay awake, when your adrenaline starts flowing when the star of the show tries to cut you to shreds in front of the entire cast and crew. But that's also why I always bring an extra pair of underwear."

Max from Zurich: "Who was the guy?"

"After all that, after everything I've just told you, all you give a shit about is who was the guy? Fuhgetaboutit."

Max: "But who was he?"

"I'm not going to tell you."

Max: "Why won't you tell us?"

Chorus: "Yeah, tell us."

"I'm not going to tell you because it doesn't matter. I never name-drop an actor I'm talking about, because I want you to focus on what I'm trying to teach you here. That and the fact that if I trash someone, I don't want it ever getting back to them and then back to me."

Max: "Yes, but if you give us the name, it will be easier for us to remember the lesson."

"Let me think about it for a minute. Ahhhhh . . . no. And hey, Max from Zurich? You know I love you because you've shot some very good film. But you wanna survive this class? Here's a little extra-credit homework for you to do: Remember that Swiss girl from Basel I told you about, the one I dated in college? Find her. Find Beatrice. Tell her I still love her. Tell her to come home."

A TOAST TO LEROY

DAD'S SEVENTY-FIFTH birthday is coming up. His wife, Susan, is throwing a party at their house and she's asked some of us to give a toast to Dad.

There are many people at the party who I don't know. Bill Shatner is there and I can't think of a single instance where he remembered who I was when our paths crossed. And so, when I see him, I usually go up to him and shake his hand vigorously and say, "Mr. Shatner, I'm one of your biggest fans!" Or when I'm really putting him on, I'll say, "Mr. Shatner, you're one of my biggest fans!" because people on the street would get so excited, they'd say that to Dad all the time. And then Bill will look at me like he thinks he should know me from somewhere but just can't quite place the face. That's when I put him out of his misery and introduce myself.

After dinner, the speeches start. I'm up after my sister. She talks about how much she enjoyed joining dad in some of his hobbies, like photography, and how much fun it was back in the '70s to fly across country with him in his single-engine plane. When it's my turn, I begin by saying a few brief things about my life with Dad, like how sweet it was to be in that Christmas Parade the first year *Star Trek* aired, after we didn't even make the cut as bystanders the year before.

"Another memory that I always find amusing is that in one of the first newspaper articles on Dad, the reporter repeatedly

referred to him as Leroy Nimroy. And Julie and I always loved
that name and sometimes when we would talk about Dad,
we'd refer to him as Leroy. And so, when I think about the life
of Leroy Nimroy, the first thought that comes to mind is that
he is a true Renaissance man. An actor, a director, a writer,
a photographer, a pilot, a recording artist, an art collector, a
philanthropist, and an all-around handyman. On Father's Day
a couple of years ago, I gave him a complete tool kit to use in
the New York apartment. Two weeks later, he calls just to tell
me how many times he's already used it. Mr. Fix-It. Mr. Home
Improvement.

"Dad was also a very good pilot, and he learned to fly in the
UK in the early seventies when he was making a TV movie over
there. And he put in enough flight time to get an instrument
rating, which essentially means you can fly the plane by instru-
ments alone when there's poor visibility. And I never once felt
any fear when I was flying with him. One of my favorite memories is when he picked up Julie and me from UC Santa Barbara,
where we were both going to school. He flew up on a Saturday
morning to take us home for the weekend. The airport is right
next to campus, which is very convenient, but it was raining
heavily that day and the runway was flooded. On the first try
at takeoff, we literally skidded sideways down the runway and
I was like, 'Dad, maybe we ought to wait till it clears up and
the runway dries off.' But a little water was not going to stop
Leroy Nimroy and he turned right around and made a second
attempt and in minutes we were airborne.

"One of the things I always admired about Dad was that he
was very patient with the fans. He was always willing to take
the time to give an autograph or have his picture taken. And
I remember when we were walking through some airport in
the early seventies, an attractive woman threw herself at him

and started kissing him. As I said, Dad was *very* patient with the fans.

"There was one time when I did see Dad lose his cool and Dad, I'm wondering if you even remember this. We were in Las Vegas—I think it was that trip to see Nancy Sinatra. We also saw Johnny Mathis and we were seated at a table right next to the stage, we were so close we could see the sweat on Johnny's forehead. Sitting next to us was a couple in their fifties and they were clearly bombed and anytime there was a pause in the middle of a song when Johnny would take a breath, this couple would jump in and say things like, 'You never sounded better, Johnny,' or, 'Your voice is like gold, Johnny, just like gold.' And once, when he was near the end of a song, in a very emotional crescendo and you could see Johnny was really in the moment, he paused, and this couple started in, 'We'll always love you, Johnny.' 'Yeah, Johnny, forever.' And it was so ridiculous that even Johnny had to laugh. And during the intermission, the guy leans over and puts his hand on Dad's arm and slurs something like, 'Wasn't Johnny terrific? Mr. Nimoy, we are very big fans of your show.' And Dad turns to this guy and with a real tough voice says, 'Sir, get your hand off my arm.' I had never seen Dad do anything like that before, and for a minute I thought there might be some real trouble. But this guy immediately realized Leroy meant business because he backed down right away.

"And I want to talk for a minute about Dad's theater career because he played so many great roles, my favorites being Theo van Gogh, Vincent's brother, in his one-man show, and Tevye in *Fiddler on the Roof,* which I really loved because he did that play as summer stock on the East Coast and it was like being in a traveling circus with this crazy, zany group of very talented people. Dad was so much fun to watch and always seemed to really enjoy playing that role. And I was also a huge fan of his work in *Man in the Glass Booth* and *Equus,* because those were easily some of the greatest performances I have ever seen in my life.

"And in terms of his recording career, well, if it weren't for Dad and Bill, we wouldn't have *Golden Throats* and the huge cottage industry that has sprung up from that.

"And I just want to finish by saying that Dad has been a huge inspiration to me in my own work. I teach directing now and my students are always caught up with the technical side of filmmaking. And what I tell them is exactly what Dad told me when I started my own directing career. On my first television episode, Dad sat down with me and we broke down the entire script. And just like my students, I started by asking, 'Where does the camera go?' Dad replied that all first-time directors get obsessed with the camera: 'Where does the camera go? Where does the camera go? Where does the camera go?' And then he said, 'The camera goes where the camera goes. The real question is, *what is the scene about?*' And I can't overemphasize the impact the gift of that simple lesson has had on my life. Because once you figure out what the scene is about, once you dig deep to discover what's really happening in your story and in the scene, then where the *characters* go becomes clearer and where the camera goes to capture the action of the characters becomes increasingly apparent. And that advice has been my mantra for years and it has served me very well both on the set and in the classroom.

"So Dad, for that and for all the roads we've traveled and all the experiences we've shared together, here's to you on your seventy-fifth. I love you and wish you many more healthy and productive years to come."

NUMBER NINE, NUMBER NINE, NUMBER NINE

WHEN I FIRST moved out of the house, during the early days of my recovery, I would often wake up in the morning feeling down and broken, thinking about all the things that had happened, all the things I had said and done, all the mistakes I had made, all the things I had lost—mostly about the things I had lost—mostly about the failure of my marriage and about not being at the house with Maddy and Jonah.

I would then roll out of bed and to make myself feel better I would take my old man out of the closet in my mind and give him a good thrashing for all the hurtful things he has said and done through the years, all the injustices. Day after day, I would go through the litany in my head and judge and criticize and condemn him. All to make myself feel better. It's amazing how some of us hold on to our hatred and resentment just to make ourselves feel better. It's taken these past three years of the step work and the meetings and the commitments and the shares to begin to steer away from that habit, to try to reconfigure the warp in my mind.

Not long ago, Dad sent me a six-page letter containing a long list of complaints dating back twenty years. I was shaking as I read it. I filed it away and did what I usually do these days when confronted with this type of situation: I did nothing. "Don't just do something, sit there." "Restraint of pen and tongue" is another AA saying. His letter was just too overwhelming, and I didn't want the negative engagement that we've had so much of in the past.

My brethren in AA were supportive of my do-nothing approach. But things were churning inside me, and it didn't feel good. Maybe I was wrong. Maybe I should have taken "contrary action" and made an amends to him right away. He was clearly very unhappy about a lot of things and maybe, once again, it may have had little to do with me—or not. I don't know. I can't be sure.

Weeks later, since we hadn't talked in some time, I called Dad on my birthday just to say hi and check in with him. After we got through the niceties, he immediately asked if I was going to respond to his letter. I told him I wasn't really sure how to respond as it contained grievances going back twenty years.

"We've been through all this before and in the past it's only led to more conflict, so what's the point? We only have so much time together, Dad, and going back to the anger and resentment and mistakes and miscommunications seems like such a waste."

"Don't you have a list of things you think I did or didn't do?"

"Oh, yeah, I have a list, just as long as yours if not longer. But I'm in a place now where I really don't care anymore. These things have nothing to do with the here and now and I'd rather just let them go and move on. The fact is, there are some things on your list that *were* mistakes I made and I do take responsibility for them. But all I can say is, I'm sincerely sorry."

"Which mistakes are you referring to?"

"I'm not going to say because I don't think it really matters. The stuff that happened in the eighties and nineties, there's really nothing I can do about those things except to honestly say that I'm sorry."

When I say stuff like this, when I don't try to take him head-on, when I tell him I care about him and want to try to reconnect with him, the Tenement Street Kid from Boston usually goes silent, while he seems to be processing the information. But I know he isn't satisfied with any of this because his anger and resentment keep coming back.

"What do you want, Dad? Just tell me what you want."

"I want clarity about some of the things that have been going on over the past twenty years."

————

Several months pass. Last week, Chris Kelton called to check in and find out what was going on. I told him I was finishing my book but was still wrestling with some of the stuff about my dad. He suggested I think about using the fourth step and the ninth step as a way to approach the issues. I told him I wanted to reread those steps and think about it.

Then he called me the next day to say he'd been up in the middle of the night thinking about all this. He said he'd been thinking about the six-page letter my dad sent me. I told Chris that I already made a blanket amends for those things, that I didn't want to go into detail with my dad about all the issues, but that I sincerely apologized for hurting him.

Chris said that the best way to make a ninth-step amends is to go through the letter with my dad and let him have it out, let him get it all out. He said that I should sincerely apologize for each and every grievance and resentment my father has against me even if it's unfair or exaggerated or totally fabricated. The point is to let my dad get his feelings out and deal with his resentment, which would then hopefully allow him to start to have positive feelings toward me. Chris firmly believed that this was the only way to set him free and, in the end, to free myself.

In a way, this kind of made sense to me.

But in another way, it made me sick. Chris went on.

"In terms of your own recovery and in dealing with an issue that has dogged you all your life, I think you should sit down with him and let him go through the entire list and anything else he has to say and make your amends. In the strictest sense, it's the most effective way to do your ninth step. Even if it's difficult for you now, in the end, it's to your benefit."

I'm listening to this while I'm trying to put gas in my car and no matter how many times I try, the pump is not working properly and I'm getting very agitated.

"Chris, I hear what you're saying and I gotta think about this, because this is really painful for me and I'm not sure I can do it. Really, I hear you and I know you're probably right. The problem I'm having is that I've done this before. I've gone to his house several times to try and patch things up and it never changes anything, I just can't seem to get through to him."

"But this is different because you're in recovery now. Don't go over there with any expectation of changing him. Your goal is simply to try and make him feel better. This really is more about you than it is about him."

"Okay, I get it, I really do, and I know you're right, but I gotta hang up right now and catch my breath."

I hang up and focus on breathing. When I've settled down, I try the gas pump again and it starts working.

Then I call Justin.

"I totally disagree with doing that with your dad."

"What? Why?"

"You're going to go through your entire list of grievances with your father?"

"No. Chris says I should let my dad go through *his* list with me from that letter he wrote and that I should make a sincere and honest amends for everything and anything he throws at me."

"Ohhhh . . . Interesting . . . I totally agree with doing that with your dad."

"You do? I'm not sure I can do it. I'm not sure I can take it."

"Yes, you can. You've come a long way, and I can honestly tell you, my friend, this is going to lift a huge weight off your shoulders. And, of course, your dad will feel a lot better too, once he lets it all out and takes a giant dump."

When I called Dad to suggest we go through the letter, he jumped at the chance. And so on Friday, after teaching at the film school, I was set to go to his house and make my amends. That morning when I woke up, it was raining. It hadn't rained in L.A. that heavily for months. Of course the rain came immediately *after* the Malibu and San Diego fires, so now we had to deal with the mudslides. I rolled out of bed and opened my door to the garden running along the side of my apartment building so that I could take in the weather. And there, foraging around for food, was a large opossum. He didn't notice me and just kept walking by as I grabbed my video camera. Such a strange creature. I've never really seen one this close for this long as they're usually nocturnal and they skedaddle the second they sense any danger. Black eyes, white snout, thick fur, rat's tail. As he walked by, he shook off the rain just like a dog or cat. It was like he was somebody's pet just out for a stroll. He paid no attention to me, his focus was solely on looking for food, like he had blinders on.

As I drove to work, I called several of my friends for some moral support and asked them to pray for me. Mitchell, my sponsor, told me I should do some praying myself before going into the meeting.

In the afternoon, I arrived early and parked nearby. I joined a lineup of cars that were parking in a restricted area and it wasn't too hard to tell that these cars belonged to crew members and that there was a shoot going on somewhere nearby. I sat in my car and pulled out my mini Big Book. I read the third-step and seventh-step prayers. A van pulled up next to me. A young production assistant rolled down his window and asked me if I needed shuttling to the location. "No, thanks," I said and showed him my little book. "I'm praying." He smiled and drove off. I flipped to some passages in the book that happened to be appropriate to my situation and then I read the Serenity Prayer in its entirety. Afterward, I felt calm and prepared and ready. It felt like what I had told my directing class I feel when I stand next to the camera and call "Action": *that all the things that I have said and done and all the things that have happened in my life have led me to this moment.*

I drove up to Dad's house. I hadn't been there in some time, and the place had changed. It was always changing, constantly being remodeled. When I stepped inside, Dad offered me his hand. I gave him a hug. He led me to a small room, the library, and we sat down on either side of a wooden table. I commented on his hair, that it was longer than usual. He told me he just had it cut, that it was even longer, that they were experimenting with it for his role in the new *Star Trek* movie.

I asked him what parts of the letter he wanted to talk about. He said I was the one who wanted to talk about the letter. I had to take a moment here, as I knew he'd been wanting to talk about the letter for months. What to do, now that this wasn't a mutual meeting, now that *I was* the one who wanted to discuss the letter. This is the kind of thing that would normally awaken my anger, and for a second, a small piece of rage entered my mind, but I quickly let it go. I noticed that the room we were sitting in was meticulously furnished, much like the rest of the house: plush white carpet, freshly painted walls, pristine white shelves containing an impressive collection of art books. Looking out the window I saw a stag's head plant hanging on the wall outside. It was perfectly placed so that it was framed within one of the windowpanes. And then there were the art books.

Written on the spine of one of the books sitting behind my father were the words "Not Afraid." I decided the best course of action was for me to simply read the letter aloud in its entirety.

As I read, as I made my way through the six pages and twenty years, I apologized for all the mistakes I had made and all the things I had said and done that were hurtful to him. I told him I was sorry for all my career mishaps that were great disappointments to him. I thanked him for all the financial gifts I had been given throughout my life. I told him I was grateful for everything I received and acknowledged, without qualification or hesitation, that he had been very generous toward me.

When I finished reading, I asked him if there was anything I could do for him to make things better. He gave me a puzzled look and told me he had everything, that he was very happy with his life, that he had made it financially when he was in his thirties and that his second marriage saved his life. He repeated that he was very happy with his life.

On my way out, he showed me some of the renovations they were making to the backyard; they were remodeling the retaining wall next to the pool. As I was leaving, I hugged him and he invited me to come to Shabbat dinner sometime.

"That sounds good, Dad," I said. "I will."

I got in my car and drove carefully home in the rain. It's

amazing how the rain can wash everything away and make the city clean again. In AA we call it keeping our side of the sidewalk clean. That's what it felt like I had done with my dad, just tried to clean up my side of the sidewalk, and it felt satisfying but very empty and sad at the same time that I wasn't really sure I was getting through to him.

"You both have a problem," business manager Bernie Francis would say. "His is understanding you, yours is in getting through to him."

It's getting to the point where I'm just not sure how important all that is anymore.

It's funny because I used to have this fantasy about my parents' first house, that dilapidated house sitting on Palms Boulevard that was our first home. I always thought that if I could just buy it and fix it up again, like Dad used to do, fix it up and sell it to a nice young couple who were just starting out, that would somehow fix everything that went wrong in my life. Like I could go back and start over and get it right for all of us. I used to have this fantasy.

———

"A couple of months ago, I gave my dad a copy of the manuscript of my book and I swear I thought he was going to disown me."

I'm sitting at a sushi bar with Marla. I met her at a meeting. She's tall with long blond hair. Justin says she has the reputation of being one of the "hotties" at the meeting.

"Hot, hot. Just because I'm thin and I have breasts they think I'm hot. I don't care about hot. What I want to know is, do you think I'm pretty?"

"Uh, *hello*. Yeeaaaah."

Marla *is* really pretty. I kept obsessing about her after she gave me her number. I kept thinking "hottie sex toy." But as our second date wears on and I'm getting to know her, it's becoming clear that we're on different paths. She's been sober for nineteen years and she's on a very spiritual path and has a great attitude and outlook on life. But she also has an apartment full of cats and crystals.

"Through my recovery, I've come to believe that my purpose on this planet is to try to help people and be loving."

I like Marla's attitude and I like the fact that she knows we're on a planet. Most people think we're just in L.A.

Marla's looking for a soul mate and wants children and I'm pretty sure she's not the one for me. But there's something very cool about the fact that I just noticed her two weeks ago and started to obsess about her and now we're eating sushi and going to a movie. And I feel I can trust her—I've been opening up to her all evening as she did with me on our first date for coffee the day before yesterday. Just coffee. Lisa Schwartz rule number one.

Although I've been telling her about my book, I never said I was Leonard Nimoy's son. And she never asked.

"I thought after he read the thing, he was going to come after me with a sledgehammer."

"So how did he react?"

"He called me to say he had no problem with anything I'd written. I couldn't believe it. He had nothing negative at all. He even complimented me on the writing. I mean, my dad's got about fifteen years of sobriety but he's never made an amends to me. And I'm not even sure he realizes I was making an amends to him when we went through that letter together."

"Maybe the fact that he's okay with the book is his way of making an amends."

Marla says this very casually as she looks at me and downs another piece of the spicy yellowtail roll. Very casual for a woman who just blew my mind. What she just said is now resonating through my entire body. Like one of her crystals. And that's when I begin to realize why this woman entered my life. My AA brethren would later tell me this was all obvious to them. But it wasn't to me. Until Marla came along.

"Did you ever think of that, that this was his amends?"

"No. That's why I have you here. That is absolutely incredible."

Okay, she's still not the one for me, but I'm feeling this intense connection to her as she's smiling.

"You're dad sounds a lot like my dad, they're from the same generation. And there is no way my dad could look at the stuff he's done and own up to it. If they had to confront everything they've done, it would be devastating. My dad would have had a nervous breakdown. It's just too overwhelming. At some point, I came to the realization that I didn't have to prove to my dad that he was wrong. Believe me, he made plenty of horrible mistakes as a dad because he had some pretty screwed-up modeling from his parents, who had some *really* screwed-up modeling from *their* parents. But once I decided to give up on trying to finally prove to him he was wrong, everything was fine between us."

TO THE END OF THE EARTH

JONAH AND I drive up to Santa Cruz to surf and visit my cousin David who's going to school at UC. It's our last morning, and before driving home we walk out to the cliff to see what the waves are doing at Steamer Lane, a world-renowned surfing spot. It's a point break sitting at the northern tip of Monterey Bay. When I was out there with Justin last year, the surfers would climb over the safety rails, walk out to the edge of the cliff, throw their boards down the twenty-foot drop, and jump in after them. From where we stood, you couldn't see the water below and the surfers would jump and disappear. It looked suicidal.

There's some wave action in the water today but not as much as usual at low tide. There are only two surfers in the water when usually it's crowded as hell. With the sun behind us, we can really see how much kelp is growing out there. We can hear the seals and see them sunbathing on a rock sitting out in the water, just past the promontory of rock that juts out from the cliffs and into the ocean. A girl in a wet suit walks by carrying a short board. She climbs over the rail and walks out to the end of the promontory—straight out to the very end where the rocks jut way out into the water. Out to the end of the earth. She throws her board in and jumps in after it. It looks scary as hell but she seems fearless, as if she does this every morning. The water is freezing, there's no one else out where she jumped in, there's kelp floating around everywhere to entangle you.

The day before, I watched Jonah surf. It was on the Cowell's Beach side of the cliff, the side where the waves are long and slow, so for beginners, it's much safer. I watched him paddle out there trying to get into a wave. It was a little frustrating because he wasn't near the start of the break, which is the best place to catch one of those long, low, easygoing waves you can ride for yards down the line. He was having trouble, and I kept frantically pointing toward the break and he finally tried to paddle out to it. I brought my binoculars and though I was high up on the cliff, I could see him very well.

I sat on the grass and watched him. I'm always watching him, always trying to be there and guide him even though sometimes he really pisses me off with too much TV and too much guitar shredding and not enough schoolwork. But I'm always trying to point him in the direction of the point break. And if he doesn't quite get there, that's okay, as long as he tries to do his best.

When my grandparents came over from Russia and settled in Boston, they wanted their sons to be college-educated professionals. And they got one in my Uncle Mel who went to MIT and became a chemical engineer and vice president at Johnson & Johnson. My grandparents didn't struggle and save so that their youngest son could pursue a career in acting. I think there was plenty of love lost when he walked out the door and moved to California. When *Star Trek* hit, I think Nana and Papa began to come around but I'm not sure Dad ever received the kind of approval he wanted and deserved—the kind they were simply not capable of giving.

"Your father's probably upset because you didn't have a brilliant legal career and you're not directing now."

"Yeah, Mom, I know those are some of the reasons why he's upset and I'm sorry he feels that way. But it is *my* life. I'm in recovery, I have a good job, my kids are doing very well. I'm pretty happy with where I am right now, and no one can take that away."

During one of the low points in our relationship, Dad wrote me that he had "come to the conclusion that unconditional love was a romantic notion." Sounds a lot like something coming out of the Vulcan side of Spock. But on this issue, I'll simply have to stand with Kirk and Bones and Jill Ireland as Leila Kalomi and do everything I can to show him otherwise. Not prove it to him, as per Marla, just show him because it seems if I can let go of the past and be helpful to my dad, everything else will take care of itself.

Jonah finally caught a piece of the break and he was up and surfing on a long wave. I could see him clearly through the binoculars and when he finished the ride, he waved to me and I gave him the thumbs-up. He didn't start at the break point and the ride wasn't very long, but he was up and that was all that mattered.

Back to our last morning before driving home. Jonah and I have finally had enough of watching the surfer girl and her death-defying rides on Steamer Lane. I put one arm around him and stretch out the other with my camera aimed at us and take some pictures: our heads close together, Jonah with his funny grin. Then we walk back to our car. And there, parked next to us, is a car with a postcard picture taped to the back window. We walk over to take a look. It's a photo of Spock giving us the "Live long and prosper" salute.

FULL CIRCLE

THINGS KEEP HAPPENING. Odd coincidences keep happening all the time and I can't tell if they're happening because I'm now sober and in recovery or if they were always happening, I just couldn't see them because I was too drunk and stoned.

I think the worst of my troubles with a television producer happened on a show when I was in withdrawal. As usual I stopped smoking and drinking while I was in preproduction and I knew I wasn't feeling right. I wasn't sleeping well and I was simply in a foul mood. When we started shooting that show, I went into total burnout mode, because being in withdrawal while working fifteen-hour days can do that to you. And on this one particular show, instead of following the Terrence Howard model for directing TV shows, I stuck it to the writer/producer. One day he came on the set and told me how he wanted a scene directed. I strongly disagreed and told him if he wanted to do it his way, he should direct it himself. He did.

Last month, I was in upstate New York checking out a college Maddy wants to attend. There were a lot of other prospective students with their parents there, and in the group of parents, there stood that producer. I couldn't believe it. I immediately went over to say hello to him and he was very friendly. Then the orientation got under way, but while I was listening to all the great things about the school, I kept thinking I should make an amends to this guy. It was like the purpose of my being at that school in the middle of the Hudson River Valley was to get my daughter in and make an amends to that producer. And what's really odd about all this is that the show on which I stuck it to that producer happened to be executive produced by the writer/director of *Crash*. In any case, I was afraid to make the amends to him. And then we became separated during the tour and I didn't see him again.

When I got back to L.A., Justin said I should pursue it, so I called the guy's production office and left word with his agent but there was no return call. Mitchell, my sponsor, told me to write an amends letter and send him a draft to look at. I wrote that I was going through some personal stuff when I directed his show and apologized for acting inappropriately. I wrote that I thought the producer was a very good writer and that if there was anything I could do to make things right, to please contact me. I wrote that because that producer had once played Jesus onstage in New York, I hoped he'd be willing to accept my amends. Mitchell made me take out the Jesus part.

The producer wrote back that the events of that show were ancient history and wished me well. Again it felt like I was just keeping my side of the street clean and it was totally liberating.

————

Last night I went to the Saturday night meeting with Justin. It was held in an old house that is dedicated to AA meetings around the clock. It was a speaker meeting, and while this young Brit went on about his drinking and drugging days in the UK, I noticed a woman sitting directly in front of me. I couldn't see her face. She had very light brown hair, almost blond, and it was straight and pretty. She turned around, recognized me, and smiled. It was Rae, the girl who was with me and my parents at Bernie Taupin's party thirty years ago. When the speaker was finished, Rae and I stood up and hugged.

"You look really good," she said.

"So do you."

"What have you been up to?" she asked.

"I'm writing a memoir and you're in it."

"Really?"

"The Bernie Taupin party."

"When you threw up on Sunset Boulevard?"

"That's the one. You took very good care of me that night."

"I was so nervous, I didn't know what I was doing. When we got you home, your father put you on your bed and you were quoting Nietzsche. Nietzsche and Neil Young."

"My Nietzsche and Neil phase."

"You were delirious. You were also calling for Jerry Garcia. Jerry and your father."

"My father was right up there with Jerry Garcia? Huh. Fascinating. You know, I woke up in the middle of the night calling your name but you were gone. The next day you were incredibly sweet to me. I had taken a shower, washed all the puke out of my hair. We were standing outside by the pool. You were holding me."

"I nursed you back to health?"

"Something like that."

"You promised me a copy of that picture they took of all of us at Bernie's. I still want it."

"No!"

We laughed and I promised to scan a copy and send it to her. I kept it from her because not long after the Taupin affair, Rae dumped me in the most unceremonious way. I had done something similar to a girl four years before, so I guess it was just payback. But I kept the picture anyway.

Rae was actually my next-door neighbor when I lived with my parents at the house in Westwood but we didn't start dating until my sophomore year in college. Her parents divorced and her mother died of complications due to alcoholism. Rae has been sober for three years and divorced a year. We exchanged phone numbers.

————

This morning, I get a call from my sister. She's spending the week in New York, staying in my mother's apartment.

"How's it going out there?"

"Well, the apartment's a mess, as usual."

"What are you talking about? I went through every room when I was out there with Maddy. I went through that entire linen closet. Did you know Mom has towels from, like, a dozen different sets? She doesn't get rid of anything."

"That's our mother! Where would she be without us?"

"Julie, where would *we* be without *her*?"

"I know, I know, you're right. No, the linen closet looks good but the kitchen was a mess and I had to reorganize the whole thing. You know me, I like my kitchens clean."

"Yes, you do!"

"Listen, before I forget, I want to tell you that when I got here, there was a letter for you left with the doorman."

"A letter? From who?"

"It's from Beatrice."

JACKSON AND US

MY DIVORCE BECAME final in September 2006, just in time for Rosh Hashanah. I got the call from my attorney. "Happy new year, your marriage is over."

It was sad and scary and strange all at the same time. It still amazes me that there was so much that brought Nancy and me together in the first place and so much that we lost along the way. Now I'm just feeling relieved that I can begin a new phase in my life.

Before Nancy signed the settlement papers, she sent me a flurry of hate e-mails with several Yiddish curses thrown in for good measure. Instead of trying to force her to sign, I called her and told her that it was time for both of us to get past this phase and move on. I told her that she shouldn't worry, we were going to be friends for the rest of our lives and that I would do the best I could to make sure she was always all right.

She started crying.

"Just tell me again everything's going to be okay."

"It's not going to just be okay, it's going to be great. We both still have much to look forward to. We will always be family. There will always be the family gatherings. And whomever you're dating will always be welcome. I'll even take him skeet shooting."

This seemed to make her feel better and she told me she

loved me and I said the same to her. And I meant it. But it's funny how saying this to her means something so different now than it did when we were married.

And now that we've moved past the divorce, we have, once again, gone back to being friends. Me and my ex, my ex and me.

It's good for the kids that Nancy and I still get along. And though some members of my family don't seem to understand why I maintain my relationship with her, I don't really give a damn. It's not like we'll be getting back together. It's not like it's keeping Nancy from dating or stopping me from chasing loose women.

———

It's the springtime again. Jonah turned fifteen and man that kid is getting tall.

"You're changing," I said to him several weeks ago as I was dropping him off after school and we were walking up to the house.

"You mean I'm getting smarter?"

"Not with that D in biology you're not. I mean your body's changing."

Not only is he getting taller, but I could see that his mouth is different, his mouth and his teeth. He's older now. In the past two weeks alone, I've seen him change. He's definitely not the boy he was on our trip up to Santa Cruz just months ago. He's finishing his first year at Santa Monica High and he's actually doing better than in his days in middle school, now that he's figured out that homework is supposed to be turned in. And he's been in guitar class blowing them away, because his guitar work just keeps getting better. There's going to be another benefit concert for the Santa Monica Malibu School music program. Once again, Jackson Browne will be playing.

I'm reminded of when we all went to see Jackson play that out-door benefit two years ago and how Jackson pulled me out of that embarrassing moment between me and my kids and that blond bombshell who sat down next to me and I'm thinking, *Yeah, that's when we put the kibosh on* that *situation, me and Jackson, Jackson and me.*

This year, Jackson has decided to invite some of the guys from the guitar class, including Jonah, to sit in on a few songs at the concert. The boys in the class have been rehearsing with Jackson for weeks, and when I pick Jonah up after school, it's Jackson said this and Jackson said that. Now, it's *Jonah* and Jackson and Jackson and Jonah.

The day of the concert, we're sitting around waiting for the twelve o'clock sound check for the show that night. This year, the concert's being held in Barnum Hall, the school auditorium that's been completely refurbished and now really looks like a concert hall. I'm sitting third row center with my video camera to film the rehearsal and the boys are outside playing guitars while we wait for everyone to show up. Nancy's sitting in front of me and we're so bored waiting that we actually get into an argument. It's been months since the divorce was final and things have settled down considerably, so I guess we're due to go a few rounds. I don't even know what the hell we're fighting about, but I'm thinking to myself, *How did I let myself contribute to getting into this?* And while Nancy's really going at it, I find myself wondering whether or not I ever made a proper amends to her for all that pot smoking I did during the course of our marriage. I did send her an e-mail amends, but I'm not sure that really counts. After the Therapy Police episode, I made a halfhearted amends to her over the phone but then reminded her of our mediation appointment the following week and that prompted her to tell me to f--- off,

so I'm not sure that one really counts either. Note to myself:
Must ask my sponsor about this.

The fight with Nancy is in full swing, and we're really getting into it—the mud and the insults are flying from both sides,
when suddenly, the lone figure of Jackson Browne appears onstage. Just in the nick of time. Just like at the concert two years
ago. And we're back to me and Jackson.

Nancy runs out to get the boys. Band members and technical people start to arrive and the rehearsal gets under way.
Jonah's finally up there with all his friends as Jackson runs
through a long list of incredible songs.

As for the fight with Nancy, I figure I'll have the last word
later at the show because I happen to know that she has seats
in the mezzanine while I'm sitting in the twelfth row. That
night, before the show, she starts complaining about having to
sit upstairs. So as a consolation, I give her my binoculars.

When the concert starts, I get a text message from her asking
if there are any seats nearby. I gleefully reply, "So sorry, but
no." Now I'm really enjoying my twelfth-row seats, even if they
are all the way over to the left aisle. And this year, I don't have
to worry about blond bombshells sitting next to me because
(1) Jonah's onstage, (2) Maddy's upstairs sitting with Nancy,
and (3) to my left is the aisle and to my right is my mother.
My phone starts vibrating again with another text message.
It reads: "Turn around." I get a little agitated because I know
what's coming. I turn around and there, two rows behind me,
are Nancy and Maddy. And they're waving to me all excited.
Nancy sticks her tongue out at me.

The show just rocks. The band backing up Jackson is outstanding. And Jonah looks great up there, sitting with his buddies in a row of acoustic guitars while Jackson stands in front
of them at the mic. Jonah has a little step-out solo during one

of the songs and he's wailing away. But then I notice that he's chewing gum, he's freaking chewing gum while he's playing, and it's really annoying. I know he sees me because he knows where I'm sitting, and now I'm standing in the aisle against the wall and when he looks my way I desperately try to signal him to *close his mouth*. But he keeps chomping away. Then I notice that Nancy and Maddy are no longer behind me, they're dancing with the crowd in the center section right in front of the stage. And just at that moment, just when I want to throttle somebody because I'm pissed off about Jonah chewing gum and Nancy snaking up front and the argument that afternoon, in that exact moment Jackson starts playing "Take It Easy." Only this time, he's singing it to Nancy and Maddy, who are dancing right in front of the stage.

But because I'm still basically your run-of-the-mill self-centered drug addict, I know Jackson really means it for me.

The next day, I go over to the house and we recap the highlights from the night before because it really was an incredible show. David Crosby also performed and played some of his hits from the Byrds all the way through to Crosby, Stills, Nash & Young. We're standing in the living room and I pick up an acoustic guitar and start playing "Take It Easy." Jonah picks up another guitar and joins in. Nancy sits down and plays it on piano. Maddy's there and we're all singing and playing and doing what we used to do before I moved out of that house three and a half years ago. While I'm strumming away, I'm thinking about how far we've all come, that we're miles away from that day on the beach when Jonah cried and cried and that night in the car when Maddy grabbed my steering wheel and kept yelling at me.

In a year's time, you won't be able to recognize yourself. That's what Paula said when this all began.

And while we're playing, it feels a little nostalgic and maybe a little weird to be here. But it's all right now. It's all right because we're still playing music and singing songs just like we used to. And yes, hopefully, someday, Nancy and I will be with other people and then we'll just have to see how it all plays out. But for right now, it's all right because we're still family and we can still do things together.

And today, at this moment, while we're having so much fun playing and singing, it's just us and Jackson and Jackson and us.

ACKNOWLEDGMENTS

MANY THANKS TO Susan Reynolds who believed and pointed me to Sandra Dijkstra and to Sandra for pointing me to Dan Smetanka and to Dan for pointing me to Anthony Ziccardi at Pocket Books. Much gratitude goes to Anthony, my editor, Mitchell Ivers, and the entire staff at Pocket. Thanks also to Diane Johnson, Randee Marullo, and Mary Ann McQueen for reading and commenting, and to Melissa Benson for keeping me on point. My gratitude also to Douglas Dutton for his enthusiasm and to Jeff Herman for his negotiating skills. And my deep appreciation to Jack Grapes and The Los Angeles Poets and Writers Collective for showing me the way.

Thanks to all those who read and commented on early drafts of this book including Karen Bullis, John Carr, Nancy Forner, Meredith Freeman, Walt Gardner, Bennett Graebner, John Keller, and Joel Kliaman. Thanks also to Joe and Darlene Lacey of Maidenwine and Ed McNally and the Robert Perkins Estate for supplying some of the photos for this book.

I also want to convey my deep appreciation to my mother and father and sister Julie for giving me permission, my children for giving me everything, Nancy for holding down the fort and helping me with the photos despite the fact she's the ex-wife in this story, my colleagues and students at the New

York Film Academy for challenging me, my landlord for keeping the peace, Danny Plotkin for pushing, Ed Marshall, Chris Martin and Laura Spain for guiding, Kieran Beer for supporting, David Adler for listening, Leslie Rutledge for advising, Leah Johnson for calling, Elaine Robinson for crying, Neil and Pegi for exemplifying, The Santa Monica Public Library for existing, and Messrs Hewson, Evans, Clayton, and Mullen for bringing home the dilithium crystals.

ABOUT THE AUTHOR

ADAM NIMOY was born in Los Angeles, California, to Leonard and Sandra Zoberblatt Nimoy. He attended the University Elementary School, a "lab school" run by UCLA, where he was the subject of numerous psychological experiments. Experimentation continued at UC Berkeley in the form of mind-altering substances. In a state of mental confusion, Nimoy attended Loyola Law School where he learned that he would never get rich practicing law. In a brief moment of clarity, Nimoy left the law to study filmmaking at UCLA Extension and acting with Jeff Corey. After directing over forty-five hours of television, including episodes of *NYPD Blue*, *The Practice*, and *Gilmore Girls*, Nimoy's television career abruptly ended due to drug and alcohol addiction and other personality defects.

"They never complain about the work, just the attitude."
—Richard Weitz, agent, Endeavor.

On January 1, 2004, Nimoy entered a 12-Step program hoping to achieve a major attitude adjustment. He now teaches directing at the New York Film Academy at Universal Studios.

Nimoy lives in Santa Monica, California, where he is spotted around town whenever possible with daughter Maddy, eighteen, and son Jonah, sixteen.